A Photographic History of Cambridge

The MIT Press   Cambridge, Massachusetts   London, England

A Photographic History of Cambridge

Patricia H. Rodgers, Charles M. Sullivan,
and the Staff of the Cambridge Historical Commission

This book was set in Mergenthaler VIP
Bembo by Achorn Graphics and printed
and bound by Halliday Lithograph in the
United States of America.

Library of Congress Cataloging in
Publication Data

Sullivan, Charles M. (Charles Manning),
1940–
  A photographic history of Cambridge.
  Bibliography: p.
  1. Cambridge (Mass.)—History—
Pictorial works.
2. Cambridge (Mass.)—Description—
Views. I. Cambridge Historical
Commission. II. Title.
F74.C1S85 1984 974.4′4 84–11274
ISBN 0–262–53057–0 (pbk.)

Contents

Foreword

In the beginning the name of the place was Newtowne—one of the rural communities the Massachusetts Bay settlers created in the course of their spread west from Boston. It acquired its present name in recognition of the college the colony planted in its midst. That name was symbolic of the relationship between town and college that persisted in the centuries that followed. That relationship was not always easy, not free of tension; but on the whole it was mutually beneficial.

By the time the earliest photographers appeared, the village had become a city and the college had become a university. The first photographs in this collection were exposed some two hundred years after the founding of Cambridge. But between 1844 and 1869 Cambridge still displayed many aspects of a rural, rustic character reflected in the leisurely pace of these images. The distance from the metropolis in Boston was substantial, not only in terms of miles but also in terms of difficulty of travel; and the university was still small, enclosed within its own orbit at the square.

Between 1869 and 1894 the city passed through a rapid process of industrialization. Harness makers were evidence of survivals of the past, but electricity had intruded and the street railway established an intimate link with Boston. Memorial Hall towered over the university, an indication that Harvard was becoming a national institution. For it was in 1869 that President Charles W. Eliot began the transformation of a provincial boys' school into a modern institution of learning.

The approaching end of the nineteenth century and the beginning of the twentieth marked an era of rapid growth. Between 1895 and 1914 other sections acquired characters of their own, distinct from that of Harvard Square. The pictures of Central Square, East Cambridge, and Magazine Beach show thriving communities; the Polish wedding is a reminder that the city had ceased to be only Yankee and Irish. By the twentieth century there was a more diverse population with people from other parts of Europe, the Caribbean, and Africa.

The closing chapter deals with a period of transition, dominated by the changing character of Harvard and the Massachusetts Institute of Technology, now institutions of international importance. Many of the earlier themes—academic, immigrant, transportation, and architectural—continue, each providing a significant contribution to the transformation of the city over the span of a century.

A Photographic History of Cambridge chronicles the earliest years of photography in Cambridge up to 1945. The diverse images reflect developments in photography as well as in the urban scene. This is more than a picture book, it is a visual history of an unique city.

Oscar Handlin

≈

Acknowledgments

This book represents the cooperative effort of many people and institutions. This publication had its roots in the photo search project sponsored by the Cambridge Historical Commission in the spring of 1980. As a result of that search, more than 2,000 photographs from private collections were copied, using equipment and film donated by the Polaroid Corporation, and the images added to the Commission's archive of more than 20,000 photographs of architectural subjects and street scenes. Fifty of these photographs were selected to form a photo exhibit, Recollections of Cambridge, that traveled throughout Cambridge as part of the city's 350th-anniversary celebration during 1981–82.★ Eighty-five photographs chosen from the Cambridge Historical Commission's archive, as well as from other local collections, are the basis for this publication.

Three sources in particular have given encouragement and support since the photo search. The Cambridge Savings Bank, at the urging of senior vice-president and treasurer Lynn Chase, provided financial assistance for research and supported this publication in observance of the 150th anniversary of the bank. Mrs. Edwin H. Land provided crucial funding at the inception of the project and again at the beginning of the publication phase, and the Polaroid Corporation donated a complete 4 x 5 copy camera system and film.

A Photographic History of Cambridge is a continuation of a publications program begun by the Cambridge Historical Commission in

★Funded in part by the Massachusetts Council on the Arts and Humanities, a state agency.

1965. Under the direction of its longtime survey director, Dr. Bainbridge Bunting, the Commission produced the five-volume *Survey of Architectural History in Cambridge* over a twelve-year period ending in 1977. Robert Bell Rettig, at the time Secretary of the Commission, wrote *Guide to Cambridge Architecture: Ten Walking Tours* in 1967. These publications are based on the Commission's inventory of all 13,000 Cambridge structures and its extensive documentation of many aspects of Cambridge history. A municipal agency, the Commission has enjoyed the support of the City of Cambridge for a publications program that is probably not matched elsewhere in this country. Although no city funds were spent directly on this volume, it could not have reached its present form without the city's support.

Members of the Commission staff made a number of different contributions. Charles M. Sullivan, the executive director, gave overall direction to the project, guided the selection of photographs, and wrote the introduction and several descriptive texts. Susan E. Maycock, survey director for the forthcoming revised East Cambridge volume, provided the text for the photographs of that area. Paul T. Bockelman, assistant director, was particularly helpful with grant proposals. Arthur Krim, former survey director, wrote the text for figure 67.

The Commission was fortunate in having the aid of academic interns at key stages of the documentation process. John Borden Armstrong, professor of history at Boston University, arranged for an intern in 1979–80 and again in 1982–83. Anne Paper did most of the initial documentation of images obtained through the photo search and started the inventory of Cambridge photographers. Sharon R. Jacoby carried on the inventory and prepared the chapter on George K. Warren. Betsy Huber, an intern provided by Professor Margaret Henderson Floyd, chair of the Fine Arts Department at Tufts University, also assisted with the inventory.

Kim Withers Brengle, a research assistant hired through the National Trust/Yankee Intern program, wrote nearly half the texts. Rachel King of Brown University assisted with the final research efforts, and Catherine Hughes provided editorial assistance in the final stages of the manuscript. Maria Muller, a freelance photographer and proprietor of Silverprint, a custom darkroom service, reproduced the photographs for both the exhibit and this book.

We are grateful to the staffs of the following institutions for their time and patience: The Cambridge Public Library, the Harvard University Archives, the Boston Athenaeum, the Society for the Preservation of New England Antiquities, the New England Historic Genealogical Society, and the Boston Public Library. We particularly would like to thank three people who went out of their way to provide information: Robin McElheny, curatorial associate for visual collections, Harvard University Archives; Sally Pierce, curator of the print department of the Boston Athenaeum; and Mack Lee.

We must give credit as well to the people who preserved these images, who took the time and initiative to locate the photographs, either in their family collections or in institutional archives, and then generously lent them to the Cambridge Historical Commission. Many of them also provided background information essential for placing the photographs in historical perspective.

Finally, these images serve as a lasting tribute to the skills of the people who took these photographs so many years ago.

Patricia H. Rodgers

findings in 1839. When news of Daguerre's success reached London in January, Talbot immediately arranged a lecture at the Royal Society, in which he exhibited his images and described the process by which they were achieved. Talbot's methods were disseminated quickly, first through the journal of the Royal Academy and then through the popular press. They were first published in America in April 1839 in the *Journal of the Franklin Institute* in Philadelphia. Daguerre, on the other hand, kept his methods secret until August, after the French Chamber of Deputies granted him an annuity.

Daguerre's first announcement stimulated attempts by scientists and amateurs to emulate his success, but descriptions of Talbot's process brought the first results. By the end of 1839 both methods were well established. Although Talbot's was the first to be employed in America, because of poor quality it did not generate the popular response accorded the daguerreotype. Talbot's process was more accessible to the amateur, but Daguerre's gained commercial acceptance.

Boston, one of the first cities to receive the exciting news, was the site of much experimentation by the scientifically inclined. Two undergraduates at Harvard, Edward Everett Hale and Samuel Longfellow, were among the earliest to achieve success. Soon after the publication of Talbot's methods, Hale and Longfellow, then both seniors, produced an image in Hale's dormitory room.

Mr. Samuel Longfellow . . . and I, were intimate friends, in Massachusetts Hall in Cambridge. We . . . followed Talbot's directions as closely as possible. With these directions, and with an artist's camera, which I have still, I took a picture of the windows opposite, in Harvard Hall. In especial, there was a bust of Apollo in the window, which came out very well, . . . the bust being white on the black of the room beyond. I thought at the time, and I think now, that this was the first experiment in a Talbotype, which was made in this country.

This image has not survived. Hale continued with photography for only a short time after leaving Harvard; he also experimented with daguerreotypes, making a portrait of himself that he considered the first to be taken in Boston.

Another early experimenter who had Cambridge associations was Josiah Parsons Cooke. In 1842 at the age of fifteen, he made Talbotype images of several Boston buildings. Cooke was admitted to Harvard two years later, and several negatives of Harvard buildings made then survive in Houghton Library; these are the earliest known surviving photographs taken in Cambridge and may be the earliest surviving American Talbotype negatives. Cooke became a professor of chemistry at Harvard at twenty-three but did not participate further in the development of photography.

The exciting results produced by the early experimenters generated interest in the commercial possibilities of photography, and studios were quickly established in Boston and other major cities. As the commercial applications of daguerreotypy were limited to portraiture, most studios were located in downtown areas where foot traffic was heavy. A commercial studio—John Plumbe Jr.'s U.S. National Photographic Institute—was established as a franchise in Boston as early as

1840 and similar operations were soon set up in outlying towns such as Newport, Lowell, and Springfield. Cambridge, however, did not have a photographic studio until 1859; instead it made do with itinerant photographers. The reasons for this seeming neglect of commercial opportunity are both historic and geographic.

Cambridge was established as the capital of Massachusetts Bay Colony two centuries before the invention of photography. After a few years of excitement, the General Court removed to Boston in 1638 and the town settled into a quiet existence as the seat of Middlesex County and the home of Harvard College. Located at the intersection of major land routes to the western towns and to New Hampshire, Cambridge was an important regional center in the seventeenth and eighteenth centuries. The early events of the Revolution—the expulsion of the town's considerable Tory population, the location of the American headquarters in the town, and its role in the Seige of Boston—gave Cambridge an abiding sense of its own historical significance, despite the clear commercial and political predominance of Boston just five miles downriver.

While the political limits of Cambridge before 1810 included present-day Newton and Arlington, the settled part of the town was concentrated within a quarter-mile of Harvard Square; the total population within the present city limits in 1765, after 135 years of settlement, was only 785 plus 160 students at the college. The only land route to Boston was an eight-mile road through Brookline and Roxbury; the alternative, not only for Cambridge but for all traffic from Middlesex County, New Hampshire, and Vermont, was the Charles-town ferry. All the land between Harvard Square and the Charles River in what is now Cambridgeport and East Cambridge contained four or five houses at most.

The opening of the West Boston Bridge in 1793 changed Cambridge forever. By shortening the land route to Boston to two and one-half miles, the new bridge stimulated the development of turnpikes that diverted much traffic from Harvard Square, and by opening vast areas of pastureland to development gave rise to the new village of Cambridgeport. Construction of Craigie's Bridge just downstream in 1809 initiated the growth of a third village at Lechmere's Point, known as East Cambridge. These new centers quickly became political rivals of what had come to be known as Old Cambridge. In 1812, Old Cambridge lost the courthouse to East Cambridge, and in 1832 the town hall was moved to Cambridgeport. By this time, the differing character of these settlements was clear: East Cambridge was becoming heavily industrialized, while Cambridgeport was thriving on the commerce generated by the bridges and turnpikes. Old Cambridge, however, retained the college and the residential neighborhoods and truck farms associated with it. In the early 1840s, Old Cambridge tried to secede from Cambridgeport and East Cambridge, but the moment was past when the newer villages could be outweighed at the polls, and Cambridge gave up its town meeting to become a city in 1846.

None of the three rival villages could muster sufficient business to attract a daguerreotype studio in the 1840s, despite the many amateurs entering the trade. By 1855, almost ten years after incorporation, the population of Old Cambridge was 5,379, of Cambridgeport, 8,775, and of East Cambridge, 6,319. If this population had been concentrated in one major center, Cambridge would have had more commercial vitality and might have offered a commercial photographer more opportunity. But each village had its limitations; Harvard Square was a sleepy village with little commercial activity beyond that generated by the college. East Cambridge, a vigorous industrial center and seat of Middlesex County, was only twenty minutes' walk from the studios on Washington Street in downtown Boston. Central Square the commercial district of Cambridgeport, became a lively commercial center later in the nineteenth century; at mid-century, however, its troubles were manifold, as described in the 1849 City Directory:

This section of the city is the principal place of business, though the opening of the Quincy Market in Boston, and the construction of numerous railroads all of which by some fatality seem to avoid Cambridge, have almost annihilated the extensive trade which was formerly carried on between "the port" and the country towns, even as far back as the borders of Vermont and New Hampshire.

Another significant aspect of the relationship of Cambridge to Boston was the development of public transportation between the two centers. In 1826, hourly stagecoaches ran from Harvard Square to downtown Boston via Central Square, the first high-frequency transit route in America. Continual improvements on this route worked to the benefit of Cambridge residents and the detriment of its businesses; each reduction in travel time or increase in capacity made downtown Boston more convenient to Cambridge shoppers and discouraged the growth of an independent downtown. Improvements included the introduction of the second horsecar line in America in 1856 and the opening of the Cambridge subway in 1912.

Commercial photography finally arrived in Cambridge in the late 1850s with the introduction of the ambrotype process, a technological advance that reduced the cost of a portrait from five dollars for a daguerreotype to as little as twenty-five cents. The first recorded photography studio was that of John Stimpson, who was listed in the 1859 Cambridge Directory as an ambrotypist with a studio in Wood's Block on Main Street (now Massachusetts Avenue) opposite Pearl Street in Central Square. Stimpson appears for only one year, but the 1860 and 1861 directories each lists a studio with a different name in the same location. After four studios had come and gone in Central Square, two were established—George K. Warren's in 1863 and Frederick C. Low's in 1866—that lasted for approximately twenty years. As Low and Warren died or retired, two new men—David W. Butterfield (who first opened a studio in Boston in 1862) and Horace Webster Whitney—established studios in 1882 that operated until 1903 and 1917. During this period from 1863 to 1917, when four firms dominated the studio photography business in Central Square, thirty-four others came and went. This set the pattern for commercial photography in most of Cambridge.

Commercial photography in Cambridge appears to have been a high-risk adventure, with few long-term winners. Of the 133 commercial photographers listed in Cambridge directories between 1849 and 1944, almost two-thirds stayed in business for three years or less; more than one-third lasted only one year. Only two out of ten lasted more than eight years. Those who succeeded in staying in business tended to make a career of it; twenty-seven firms lasted more than eight years, probably for the working lives of their proprietors. One firm that passed down to the next generation, Whitney & Son of Central Square, operated in the same location for thirty-six years, and the two mainstays of college photography, Pach Brothers and Notman, lasted thirty-seven and fifty-one years. Almost all proprietors were entrepreneurs working for themselves. Commercial photography was a field in which an individual would invest a small amount, operate for as long as business was good, and then sell out the equipment, lease, and goodwill—if any—to another. In economically uncertain times, men turned to photography as a stopgap, often unaware of the skill and persistence needed for success. Improved technology lured poorly qualified entrepreneurs, who entered the business only to fail.

Commercial photographers operated in the five major business districts in Cambridge, but conditions in each differed greatly. Cambridgeport found new prosperity after the Civil War as a suburb for Boston merchants who commuted by horsecar; its business district, Central Square, had twice as many studios come and go as the next largest center, Harvard Square. By the 1920s, when the population of Cambridge had reached 120,000, Central Square was the city's unrivaled commercial center, achieving a real prosperity since lost to downtown Boston and the suburbs. Although large numbers of pho-

tographic enterprises were established there, few achieved long-term success. Between 1907 and 1930, for example, twenty-nine studios were established but only six lasted more than three years. In the wartime years of 1917–1919, six studios were founded to meet the demand from servicemen and their families; none survived the postwar depression. In each year between 1895 and 1932 at least three and as many as seven studios operated in Central Square, but there were never more than two studios dominating the trade. Cambridge in this period was a thoroughly prosperous community; it was at once a prestigious suburb, a university community, and an industrial powerhouse. The Central Square commercial studios recorded that vitality, as can be seen in many of the photographs that follow.

Old Cambridge, with Harvard Square as its center, did not have the numbers or the prosperity of Cambridgeport. But entrepreneurs realized that Harvard College provided a large if specialized market for photography, primarily among undergraduates. George K. Warren first tapped the potential of this market by selling yearbooks comprised of photographs of college and town scenes to graduating classes in 1861; at the time his studio was still located in Lowell. In 1863, Warren moved his studio to Central Square and worked there until he lost the college business in 1877. The college trade was served by others until the opening of G. W. Pach & Brothers in 1880 and James Notman in 1881. These firms lasted until 1916 and 1931, and between them dominated the New England college market for most of that time. After 1882 Pach Brothers had their studio in a Shingle Style building designed for them next to the Old Cambridge Baptist Church in Quincy Square (figure 84). The Notman Studio occupied the top floor of a nondescript commercial building on Massachusetts Avenue at Linden Street, opposite the future site of Widener Library (figure 83). Only during the World Wars, when Harvard facilities were used to train military officers, were there more than three studios in the square. To meet wartime demand, eight studios operated in 1918, and seven in 1944. Only one firm prospered through both wars and the Depression.

The other Cambridge markets were smaller and more specialized. East Cambridge, while densely settled with a large and ever-changing immigrant population, had only one studio (under three different operators) between 1865 and 1895, and then went without until 1919. Inman Square, in a neighborhood that grew from a later influx of immigrant families between 1890 and 1930, had no photographer before 1895; between 1915 and 1922, nine studios were established, almost all short-lived. Outlying Porter Square, the center of Irish North Cambridge, had only one studio for most of the years between 1890 and 1944.

Except for the firms that catered to the college trade, commercial studios seemed to depend on the talents of individual entrepreneurs and the opportunities offered by a constantly changing urban environment. As the population grew, so did the ranks of photographers, augmented in expansionary times by inexperienced hopefuls and in wartime by opportunists. By far the majority who tried their hands at

the trade failed in short order and moved on. Those who were successful made a career of it.

Although commercial photographers dominated the field until the 1890s, the accessibility of photography advanced in the 1850s with the invention of easily reproduced paper prints. In the 1860s, stereo photography became big business, aided by the invention of the first practical stereo viewer by Oliver Wendell Holmes in 1859. Stereo views of such well-known landmarks as the Washington Elm and Longfellow's house were widely distributed and are common today, but commercial photographers also made views of strictly local interest. Fred C. Low, a Central Square photographer, was working in this genre when he made a stereo view of his studio after a snowstorm in the 1880s (figure 82).

Another major advance was the use of photographs in books. In the 1850s, books were occasionally illustrated by tipping in paper prints, but this was expensive and time-consuming. By the end of the decade new gelatin relief processes patented under such names as albertype, collotype, and heliotype were used to print images directly on the page. The heliotype process was adopted by the Boston publisher Ticknor & Fields and their successors, James R. Osgood & Company; many of their illustrated books were published by Welch, Bigelow & Company, which did business as The University Press in Brattle Square.

Books of this genre often coupled romantic photographs with nostalgic descriptions of New England scenes. One of the most important was William J. Stillman's *Poetic Localities of Cambridge* (1876), a collection of twelve heliotypes illustrating as many poems by Henry Wadsworth Longfellow, James Russell Lowell, and Oliver Wendell Holmes, all nationally known Cambridge figures. The appearance of this book, following the 1873 publication of Samuel Adams Drake's *Historic Fields and Mansions of Middlesex*, was in keeping with the interest in colonial times that began with the Centennial, and marks the beginning of an obsessive concern with the Washington Elm tradition, the Tory Row mansions, and other landmarks of the Revolution that is evident in much historical writing about Cambridge. Also expressive of the period was Wilson Flagg's *The Woods and Byways of New England*, which included twenty-two heliotypes of specimen trees and rural scenes in Massachusetts, two of them in Cambridge. This was not a celebration of wilderness but a romantic pictorial of an ancient man-made landscape even then thought to be disappearing.

Photography first became a popular medium with the introduction of dry-plate glass negatives in 1880 and amateur cameras by the Scoville Company and Eastman Kodak later in the decade. Amateurs had always been active in Cambridge; now the dry-plate process separated the act of picture taking from that of negative processing, and for the first time allowed true portability. Among the Cambridge figures to make significant use of the new process was the ornithologist William Brewster (1851–1919). Leaving the private museum behind his house at 145 Brattle Street, he made thousands of images of bird habitats and landscape scenes at Fresh Pond, Waverly Oaks, the Sudbury marshes, and farther afield in Maine and New Hampshire. His work is preserved at Harvard's Museum of Comparative Zoology, the Massachusetts Audubon Society, and the Society for the Preservation of New England Antiquities, although none is included here.

Between 1885 and 1895, film technology advanced with startling rapidity. The marketing of roll film in 1885, bromide paper—sold ready for use—in 1886, transparent film in 1889, and film rolled to permit daylight loading in 1895, along with the development of inexpensive amateur cameras, meant that many people who might rarely procure a studio portrait were introduced to the practice of photography. By the late Nineties, scrapbooks began to fill with snapshots of vacation scenes, family groups, country life, pets, and children. Such scrapbook collections are of increasing interest as time provides distance from the original scenes, but too few are properly labeled to allow historians to use them.

Concurrent with advances in technology was the proliferation of clubs formed by amateur photographers. The best known of these in Cambridge was the Old Cambridge Photographic Club, formed in 1892 and so named because Cambridge Camera Club had already been established in Cambridgeport. In a history of the club written in 1903, its first president, James A. Wells, noted that "the general adoption of dry plates between 1880 and 1890 . . . so simplified and facilitated all the processes of photography that many were induced to take up the art as a recreation."

The composition of the club was characteristic of other amateur groups in Old Cambridge at the turn of the century. It was limited to twenty-five members, who were admitted by vote of the general membership; this was apparently a device to ensure personal compatibility, which in this period meant an exclusiveness not so much economic as social and geographic. Four of the seven founding members were women, and through 1902 more than one-third of the total membership were young unmarried women. Amateur photography was a young person's hobby, and the Old Cambridge Photographic Club, like the Cambridge Dramatic Club and other similar organizations of the period, was as much a means for young people to socialize as to pursue an interest in a new medium of expression.

The enthusiasm generated by the new hobby is reflected in the popularity of the club and its activities. The first of many annual exhibits was held in 1894 and attracted 293 entries, of which 250 were selected. In 1898, the club had fourteen meetings, six competitions, and an annual exhibition attended by more than 2,000. The competitions were an important activity; they were often judged by outsiders or held with rival clubs and were viewed as developing the skill and sophistication of members. The popular impact of its exhibitions was so evident that in 1896 the club entered the public debate over the improvement of the Charles River Basin. The Photographic Club's competition had as a theme the documentation of the Charles River from its source to the sea. Members were assigned a specific section of the river to photograph. The winning entries were exhibited in Cambridge, and lantern slides made from them were shown twenty-five times or more in public presentations throughout the Boston area.

The publicity campaign was sucessful, and the Charles River Basin from the new dam to Watertown Square was included in the metropolitan park system.

Only a few photographs from the Charles River exhibit have been found, but they illustrate the developing interests and skill of the members in a period when amateur photography was characterized by a soft-focus romanticism that may have been generated as much by a reaction against the sharp images of the professional's silver print as by the technical limitations of the new photographic processes. The increasing sophistication of the amateurs who made up the club is illustrated by the subjects that were awarded prizes. In the club's first exhibit in 1894, the first three prize-winning photographs were titled "Trespassers in the Berry Patch," "Little Cousins," and "Cat's Cradle"; although none have survived, the cloying imagery is apparent. Tastes developed very quickly, perhaps encouraged by the photography manuals awarded as prizes, and first place the next year went to "Distant View of Mount Chocorua" by Lois Lilley Howe.

Tension in this period between representation of detail and expression of the photographer's art was clearly recognized in Wells's history, in which he noted that the club had been

. . . founded in a happy hour, just when the old albumen silver print, with its superfluity of detail, was giving way to more artistic methods, and photographers had begun to reach out to higher ideals. . . .

The same advances that fueled the growth of amateur photography enabled organizations to record their activities without engaging a professional photographer. Large collections amassed by the Cambridge YMCA, the Cambridge Recreation Department, and the Cambridge Electric Light Company between 1900 and 1930 illustrate, in an informal way, the concerns and interests of those organizations. All hired studios to present an image to the public, but they relied on employees to capture everyday events.

Other organizations made it a practice to have a staff photographer on call. The most important commercial collection of Cambridge images is that of the Boston Elevated Railway Company from 1895 to about 1940. The Elevated was a metropolitan transit system that evolved from the numerous horsecar lines serving the Boston area in the nineteenth century. In 1895 the company began construction of the Tremont Street subway, Boston's first, and went on to build rapid transit lines throughout the region. These projects were extensively documented by large-format photography, starting with views of each structure along the proposed route and continuing with repetitive views of the progress of construction. This invaluable collection, containing approximately 10,000 images, is on deposit at Harvard University. The 1,000 negatives dealing with the construction of the Cambridge subway are being restored by the Cambridge Historical Commission as funds permit.

Public agencies often had staff photographers who recorded valuable images, although sometimes inadvertently. The photographer of the Cambridge City Engineer's Office, when not documenting progress on public works projects, would often be engaged by the city's Law Department to record a broken sidewalk, pothole, or automobile acci-

dent that caused personal injury. The street scenes thus captured would not otherwise have been preserved. The Cambridge Park Department, formed in 1892, was engaged for many years in constructing a park system designed by Charles W. Eliot and Frederick Law Olmsted. It kept an extensive photographic record, now preserved only in the halftones in its annual reports. The Metropolitan District Commission, a regional agency that took over administration of Memorial Drive from the Cambridge Park Commission in 1920, also recorded its construction projects as well as scenes in the parks, roads, and waterways under its control.

The greatest advance in photography made in Cambridge since Josiah Cooke's Talbotypes took place at the end of the period covered by this book. Dr. Edwin Land began experimenting with synthetic light polarizers in 1927, and in 1944 began working seriously in one-step photography. His laboratory was located at Main and Osborne streets in the factory building where Alexander Graham Bell made the first reciprocal telephone call in 1876. Dr. Land's experiments were successful, and the first practical Polaroid images were made on a sepia-toned film in 1946. A complete camera system was offered to the public in 1948. Polaroid has maintained its headquarters and manufacturing facilities in Cambridge to the present.

Probably the majority of the photograph collections of Cambridge subjects have now disappeared. No negative files of commercial studios are known to have survived. The companies that made Cambridge a major industrial center could be expected to have left a record of their activities, but of the best known—New England Glass, Irving & Casson–A. H. Davenport, Boston Woven Hose, American Rubber, Simplex Wire & Cable—little or nothing has survived. Families are often as thoughtless, discarding albums of portraits or scenes that no living descendant can identify but that might be invaluable to historians. Photographs are the raw material of recent history, and historians would be better served if more were saved.

The photographs in this book are a small selection from those that have found their way into the collections of the Cambridge Historical Commission and other local archives. Many were discovered during the photo search project organized by Patricia Rodgers. Others were drawn from the files of the Harvard University Archives, the Library of Congress, the Society for the Preservation of New England Antiquities, and other institutions. All are identified by date, location, and photographer, as far as these are known, and described in a historical note. It is a difficult task to describe a city as diverse as Cambridge in a selection of only eighty-five photographs, a number determined by the constraints of time and budget. We felt that the historic landmarks of Cambridge—Harvard College, the homes of Longfellow, Lowell, Fayerweather, Brattle, and Lee, and the Washington Elm—had been represented too frequently and that much of the life of the city had never been properly depicted. Our first aim was diversity of subject, scene, and neighborhood. The chronological divisions of the book reflect both advances in photography and the major periods of Cambridge's development as a city. The period from 1870 to 1894, for ex-

ample, was the time of the albumen print and the commercial photographer; it was also the period in which Cambridge grew from a semirural village to a city on the verge of modernity. The next chapter begins in 1895 with the development of amateur photography and the electrification of street railways, two advances that gave individuals new freedom of expression and movement and intensified the suburban character of the city. With the completion of the subway to Boston in 1912 a metropolitan character of intense urban activity developed. With World War II, the Cambridge scene becomes for some a memory of conflict and the Depression; images are familiar yet remote—already part of history.

Charles M. Sullivan

I Before 1869

1 *Gore Hall*

Location: Harvard Yard
Date: 1844
Photographer: Josiah Parsons Cooke
Source: Harvard University Archives

ଽ✑

Josiah Parsons Cooke was among the first experimenters in photography, and his Talbotype negatives are the earliest such images to survive. Cooke made a number of Talbotypes of Boston buildings in 1842 at the age of fifteen and continued the practice after his admission to Harvard two years later. Nine of his negative prints are held by Houghton Library. Two were taken in Boston of the Boston City Hall and Museum and the old Merchants Bank Building. Five are of Harvard buildings, including Gore, Harvard, Holworthy, Massachusetts, and Divinity halls, and two are unidentifiable. Harvard collected the images from various sources. Three of the nine were given to Justin Winsor, the Harvard College librarian, by Cooke in 1881; another came from the collection of Frederick Law Olmsted.

Gore Hall, the college library, was built in 1838 to a design by Richard Bond with a $100,000 bequest from former Massachusetts Governor Christopher Gore. At the time it was completed in 1841, it housed 41,000 books and was expected to be adequate for seventy-five years. Instead, it was overflowing in less than one-third of that time. An addition built in 1874 was notable for employing steel bookstacks for the first time. Gore Hall was demolished to make room for Widener Library in 1913 but is retained on Cambridge's city seal.

South Side of Harvard Square

Location: Massachusetts Avenue,
looking south to Harvard Square
Date: Before 1856
Photographer: Unknown
Source: Harvard University Archives

ϡ

This view, taken before tracks were laid for horsecar lines to Boston and Porter Square in April, 1856, is one of the earliest known photographs of Harvard Square. It is a striking contrast to Harvard Square today, both in the smaller scale and lower density of the two- and three-story brick and frame buildings and in the absence of heavy traffic on Massachusetts Avenue. Most of the buildings, including those of Harvard College, face into the square, indicating a close integration of the various elements of Harvard Square life in the middle of the nineteenth century.

The photograph centers on a cluster of commercial buildings, which, with the Willard Hotel visible on their left, typify the low frame buildings that still lined Harvard Square at the time. The wooden building with the broad gable front is Farwell's General Store; on the left is another frame building that housed a dry-goods store with a residence above. Both of these late-eighteenth-century buildings, now greatly altered, still stand at the junction of Massachusetts Avenue and John F. Kennedy Street.

Harvard College buildings then as now occupy the east side of Massachusetts Avenue. The oldest surviving college building, Massachusetts Hall, is visible through the trees at the far left. Built in 1718, the structure was originally a dormitory housing sixty students and one or two tutors. Since 1939, it has been occupied by administrative offices as well. To the south, the portico of Dane Hall is faintly visible. Built in 1832 to house the Law School, it was destroyed by fire in 1918.

On the other side of the street from these official college buildings stands College House, Harvard's first private dormitory, built in 1832 for law students and expanded over the years to accommodate a growing student population. The original three-story brick structure was doubled in 1845. In 1859, after this photograph was taken, a third section was added, and in 1870 a mansard roof and central pavilion completed the structure. College House served as a dormitory with commercial use at street level for many years until, eventually, commercial purposes took over completely. Parts of the building were demolished in 1916 and 1956, but most of it still stands.

The First Parish Church, which dominates the right-hand side of the photograph, was built in 1833 by the newly-formed Unitarian faction of Cambridge's Congregational worshippers. Designed by Isaiah Rogers, the church is a fine example of Gothic Revival architecture. Harvard used the First Parish Church for commencement until 1873.

The fourth courthouse, whose cupola is just visible in the distance between College House and the First Parish Church, was originally built in 1758 on the present site of the Harvard Coop. After 1816, the structure was used for town meetings until Lyceum Hall was constructed on the site in 1841. At that time the courthouse building was moved to Palmer Street, as shown in this, the only known photograph of the structure. On its new site, the former courthouse building was used variously as a billiard parlor, a bowling alley, the first gymnasium for Radcliffe College, and finally, a warehouse, prior to its demolition in 1930.

5   *Before 1869*

3 *West Side of Harvard Square*

Location: 1400-1430 Massachusetts
Avenue
Date: c.1865
Photographer: George K. Warren
Source: Stones Reprographics

૩✒

These three brick buildings are representative of the development taking place in Harvard Square in the early to middle nineteenth century. Brick construction was beginning to replace wood in commercial and public buildings. Commercial activity was increasing, encouraged by the growth of the college and the extension of horsecar lines. Horsecars, like the one at right center, had come into use in 1856, connecting Harvard Square with Boston and Porter Square. At this time the waiting room for horsecar passengers was on the ground floor of College House, the three-story brick structure at the far right. The portion of College House visible here was demolished in 1956 for the constuction of the Harvard Trust Company. The later extensions of College House to the north have survived.

The Greek Revival building in the center is Lyceum Hall, built in 1841. Its basement and first story housed the Harvard Book Store and the American Telegraph Company office; the second story was a hall used for lectures and concerts. Lois Lilley Howe remembered having attended the dancing school of Mr. Papanti in the Lyceum Hall as a child in the 1870s. The hall housed the Harvard Cooperative Society from 1918 until 1924, when the Lyceum was demolished to erect the present Coop building.

7   *Before 1869*

4 *Dane Hall*

Location: East Side of Massachusetts
Avenue, Harvard Yard
Date: c. 1865
Photographer: George K. Warren
Source: Cambridge Historical Society

ঽ❧

Built in 1832, Dane Hall was the first permanent home of the Harvard Law School. The Law School was founded in 1817, but struggled through its first decade with a faculty of two, occupying several rooms on the ground floor of Webber House. Its periodic requests for better facilities were denied, and by 1829 the school was on the verge of closing. Then Nathan Dane, a Beverly lawyer and legal author, offered Harvard $10,000 to support the Law School. With this financial backing, the school flourished. As the student population grew, the need for new facilities became more acute, and Dane provided funds for the construction of the new hall bearing his name.

Dane Hall stood south of Massachusetts Hall and faced College House across Massachusetts Avenue, built in the same year as a law-student dormitory. The orientation of Dane Hall, with its Ionic portico directed outward toward Harvard Square, was typical of many Harvard buildings prior to the beginning of the twentieth century. Several small quadrangles facing Harvard Square had been built in the eighteenth century, notably one bounded by Harvard Hall, Old Stoughton Hall (demolished in 1781), and Massachusetts Hall. Dane Hall and Massachusetts Hall formed the beginning of another quad. Oriented toward the square, this quadrangle was completed in 1871 after Dane Hall was moved seventy feet south to accommodate the construction of Matthews Hall. When the college fence and gate were built in the later nineteenth century, the focus of the college began to shift inward toward the Old Yard.

The ground floor of Dane Hall contained a library and reading room as well as studies for the Law School's two professors. On the second floor were a lecture room and two smaller rooms. A rear wing was added in 1845 for the expanding law library.

By the 1870s its occupants found Dane Hall too small, poorly ventilated, and too close to the increasing noise of Harvard Square. After the Law School moved to Austin Hall in 1883, Dane Hall housed the Harvard Cooperative Society, a psychology lab, and administrative offices until it was destroyed by fire in 1918.

5 *The Delta*

Location: Intersection of Cambridge, Kirkland, and Quincy streets
Date: c. 1865
Photographer: George K. Warren
Source: Cambridge Historical Society

ፙ

This triangle of land, defined by Cambridge, Kirkland, and Quincy streets and the present site of Memorial Hall, was known as the Delta in the early nineteenth century. The space was used for Harvard playing fields until 1870, when construction began on Memorial Hall and Jarvis Field was purchased for collegiate sports.

The block of Kirkland Street bordering the Delta had been known as Professors' Row since 1822, when Harvard sold five house lots along that road to Harvard professors. Thomas Wentworth Higginson, who grew up on Professors' Row in the 1820s, recalled "students climbing or swinging on Dr. Charles Follen's outdoor gymnastic apparatus, or perhaps forming to trot away with him at double-quick, their hands clenched at their sides, across the country." The rest of the Delta was covered with apple trees. There were no houses on Quincy Street between Professors' Row and Broadway, and between Quincy Street and Cambridgeport lay woods and open fields.

Harvard's first gymnasium, Rogers Hall, was built in 1859 adjacent to the Delta on a smaller triangle formed by Quincy Street, Cambridge Street, and Broadway. This octagonal brick structure was used as the Engineering School and later as the Germanic Museum after the original Hemenway Gymnasium was built in 1878. In 1933, Harvard exchanged this lot for the Little Common, and Rogers Hall was replaced by the fire station which still stands on the site.

11   *Before 1869*

6 *Botanic Garden*

Location: Corner of Garden and
Linnaean streets
Date: 1867
Photographer: John A. Whipple
Source: Cambridge Historical
Commission

જે

This is a portion of the Botanic Garden that was located on Linnaean Street at the corner of Garden Street. At the right is the herbarium, built in 1867, and at the left is the home of Asa Gray, then the director of the Botanic Garden. Gray's house, built in 1810, is the earliest known design by Ithiel Town, an architect who achieved national prominence for his buildings in New Haven and New York. The Botanic Garden also included a conservatory and a gardener's cottage.

The garden was established in 1805 under the sponsorship of the Massachusetts Society for Promoting Agriculture and acquired by Harvard College in 1831. The original purpose of the garden was to cultivate plants from various parts of the world, as well as indigenous flora, for experiment and instruction. The Botanic Garden achieved international fame under Asa Gray's directorship, from 1842 to 1873. Gray was known in the botanical field as teacher, author, and ardent Darwinist.

After Gray's departure, the Botanic Garden faced severe financial challenges and eventually fell into disrepair. The house was moved to 88 Garden Street, where it still stands. In 1949, Harvard faculty and veterans housing was built on the site of the Botanic Garden. The architects DesGranges & Steffian incorporated many of the specimen trees on the property into their design.

This photograph is one of a series taken by John A. Whipple for the Harvard Class Album of 1867. Whipple, a Boston photographer, achieved international prominence with his early daguerreotypes of the moon and stars taken at the Harvard Observatory.

7 *Washington Elm*

Location: Corner of Mason and Garden streets
Date: 1861
Photographer: George K. Warren
Source: Cambridge Historical Society

The Washington Elm was undoubtedly one of the most popular photographic subjects of nineteenth-century Cambridge. To the left is the Abraham Hill house with its distinctive row of poplars and to the right is the Prentice family house, both now demolished.

The Washington Elm was one of six elms planted along Garden Street around 1700. Because George Washington was once believed to have taken command of the American Army under its branches on July 3, 1775, the elm was much photographed and written about. In fact, according to Cambridge historian Samuel F. Batchelder,

Washington never did "take command" in any formal way. Washington probably assumed command on July 2, 1775, in an unceremonious manner. He may have stood near the elm on July 3 while reviewing American troops gathered on the common.

When the common was enclosed in 1830, the elm was isolated in the intersection of Garden and Mason streets. The protective iron railing, donated by the Reverend Daniel Austin, was placed around the tree in 1847. Slowly dying over a long period of time, the elm was pulled over in 1923 by workmen trying to remove a dead branch.

Today a brass marker in the middle of Garden Street and a stone marker in the common next to a scion of the original elm are the only reminders of the historic tree.

The Abraham Hill house and the Prentice house were eighteenth-century structures that were demolished in the nineteenth century. The Hill house was built about 1718 and destroyed in 1863. The Shepherd Congregational Society, later the First Church Congregational, built its second church on the Hill house site in 1871. The church, designed by Abel C. Martin, stands now as a focal point at the corner of Garden and Mason streets.

8

Oliver Wendell Holmes and His Family

Location: Holmes Place
Date: c. 1862
Photographer: Unknown
Source: Cambridge Historical Society

By the time this photograph was taken Oliver Wendell Holmes was already famous as a physician, author, and raconteur.

Born in Cambridge in 1809, Holmes was a contemporary of Richard Henry Dana and Margaret Fuller, both of whom were schoolmates, and he was a member of a Cambridge literary circle that included James Russell Lowell and Henry Wadsworth Longfellow. Holmes graduated from Harvard College in 1829 and after a tour of Europe took a degree in medicine in 1838. From 1847 to 1882, he was a professor at the Harvard Medical School, but his work as a physician did not inhibit his literary pursuits. Holmes had begun to write poetry while still an undergraduate; his *Old Ironsides* was credited with saving the frigate *Constitution* from destruction.

The Autocrat of the Breakfast-Table, which first appeared in 1831, began his reputation as an author and humorist. In 1857, Holmes was involved in establishing *The Atlantic Monthly*; he suggested the name, and James Russell Lowell agreed to be editor if Holmes would be a frequent contributor.

The photograph shows Holmes, his wife, Amelia Lee, his son Oliver Wendell, Junior, and his brother John Holmes on the lawn of the house where he was born and where John still lived. In the background behind the shed is the faintly visible rear wall of the first Old Cambridge Baptist Church, which then stood on the present site of Littauer Hall facing Harvard Square; it was moved to Porter Square in 1866 to become the North Avenue Congregational Church. The Holmes house was built before 1737 and was a famous landmark by the time it was demolished by Harvard University in 1883. In fact, the occasion of this photograph may have been the sale of the house to Harvard University after Holmes's mother died in 1862.

Holmes's son, who soon dropped the junior, was born in 1841. He graduated from Harvard College and Harvard Law School and eventually became as well known as his father, serving as an associate justice of the U.S. Supreme Court from 1902 to 1932. John Holmes, at the right, also went to the law school but stayed in Cambridge. Although not as well known as his brother, he was not without admirers. Thomas Wentworth Higginson reported that Emerson "once said of John Holmes that he represented humor, while his brother . . . represented wit."

9

The James A. Hunnewell House
Location: 6 Ash Street Place
Date: c. 1860
Photographer: Unknown
Source: Mrs. Ruth P. Gray

Mr. and Mrs. James A. Hunnewell and their daughters Carrie and Edith are sitting on the front porch of their Gothic cottage-style home at 6 Ash Street Place in this photograph. James A. Hunnewell purchased the house in an unfinished state from the builder, Oliver Hastings, in 1848, the same year he married Caroline Ivers in Dedham. The house still stands but lacks some of its original details, such as the drip molding pictured here.

James A. Hunnewell had grown up around the corner from Ash Street Place at 79 Brattle Street, where his father Charles lived and operated a carriage business. A jeweler and watchmaker, James A. Hunnewell owned a business at the corner of Harvard and Dunster streets from 1849 to 1883.

10 *Thomas Dowse House*
Location: 653-655 Massachusetts Avenue
Date: 1861–1863
Photographer: George K. Warren—
carte de visite
Source: Henry Deeks

ã≥

The Dowse House is an early residential building that still stands at the corner of Massachusetts Avenue and Prospect Street in Central Square, although it is now hidden under aluminum siding and a disfiguring storefront.

Shown here is the original three-story wooden structure built for Thomas Dowse in 1814. Born in Charlestown in 1772, Dowse was a leather dresser and wool merchant "who, in the days of his poverty, when he did not own a pair of boots, possessed six hundred books, well bound." A noted bibliophile and collector of watercolors, Dowse was a civic-minded individual who donated $10,000 for the establishment and support of an annual course of public lectures in Cambridge. Begun in 1858, the Dowse lectures still continue at the Cambridge Public Library.

The Dowse structure has served a variety of functions, first as Mr. Dowse's home and then, in 1861, at the time of this photograph, as offices of the Harvard Bank. The building now houses stores and offices.

11   *First Baptist Church*

Location: Junction of Massachusetts
Avenue, Magazine, and River streets
Date: 1866
Photographer: George K. Warren (?)
Source: First Baptist Church

ટે๛

This view south from Prospect Street across Massachusetts Avenue provides an early glimpse of Central Square. After the construction of the West Boston Bridge in 1793, Main Street, including what is now Massachusetts Avenue, formed an important link between the inland farms of Middlesex County and Boston. Central Square was the location of a haymarket and grew in commercial importance over the century.

Possibly taken by George K. Warren, this view documents the final stages of construction of the First Baptist Church, built to replace the First Baptist Meetinghouse of 1817, which was destroyed by fire in 1866. The new church, designed by S. S. Woodcock, was an imposing Gothic Revival-style structure that took full advantage of its prominent Central Square location. It was described as Cambridgeport's most ambitious church at the time of its construction, but it lasted only fifteen years. In 1881 a fire destroyed this second structure; it was replaced immediately by the present church, designed by the architects Hartwell & Richardson for the foundation of the 1866 church. The Dowse House shown in the preceding photograph is just out of sight to the left.

13 Thomas Leighton House
(Exterior and Interior)

Location: 22 Winter Street
Date: c. 1860
Photographer: Unknown
Source: Marion Pike

Located on a street lined with late-Georgian workers' cottages, this house was built in 1833 for Thomas Leighton, superintendent at the New England Glass Company from 1826 until his death in 1849. Glass manufacturing was an important early Cambridge industry, and many employees of the nearby Bay State Glass Company and the New England Glass Company lived in this East Cambridge neighborhood. Although this two-and-a-half-story house was larger than most on the street, Leighton's home was typical of these workers' cottages in having its gable end to the street and its main entrance facing a narrow side yard.

Leighton, born in 1786 in Newcastle-on-Tyne, England, worked as a master glassmaker in Belfast and Edinburgh. The New England Glass Company brought him to Cambridge in 1826. Of his seven sons, five became glass workers for the same company. His sons William and John succeeded him as superintendent.

Leighton's daughter Catherine inherited her father's house, and after she died, in 1856, several of her brothers lived there. The house remained in the Leighton family until 1890.

The identity of the two women in the photographs is uncertain. They may be the wife and daughter of one of Thomas Leighton's sons or perhaps they are Leighton's daughter Mary Ann Leighton Wallace and her daughter Ann, who was the only one of Leighton's grandchildren mentioned in his will.

14   *John and Francis J. Butler*

Location: Unknown
Date: c. 1862
Photographer: Unknown
Source: Catherine Agnes Tobey

ॐ

This daguerreotype of John Butler is one of the earliest known portraits of an immigrant to East Cambridge. John Butler was born in Ireland in 1824 and came to this country between 1853 and 1855, one of many Irish immigrants who settled in East Cambridge in the prewar period and worked as laborers in the local industries. At the time of this portrait, he and his wife, Catherine, had one daughter and three sons, the youngest of whom, Francis, is shown with his father.

Francis J. Butler was born in 1859 and grew up in East Cambridge to become assistant pastor of the Church of the Sacred Heart in 1885 and pastor in 1889. The Sacred Heart Church, built in 1876 to accommodate the needs of a growing Irish population, was East Cambridge's largest nineteenth-century church.

15 *The Munroe Sisters*

Location: Unknown
Date: c. 1855
Photographer: Unknown
Source: First Church in Cambridge,
Congregational.

ॐ

Susan and Mary Munroe were two of
the ten charter members of the Cambridge Sewing Circle. The circle was
founded on June 12, 1819, in all likelihood at the Munroe sisters' house on
James Street, and met on a monthly
basis at two o'clock in the winter and
at three o'clock in the summer.
Women members of the Shepherd
Congregational Society, later First
Church in Cambridge, Congregational, constituted the sewing circle.

The Cambridge Sewing Circle was
one of many such church groups in the
Boston area benefiting various missionary efforts. Proceeds went to the
American Board of Commissioners for
Foreign Missions, supporting missionary groups abroad as well as groups
serving American Indians. The first
money raised by the Cambridge ladies'
sewing efforts, a total of ten dollars,
went to a missionary group sailing to
the Sandwich Islands in 1819.

II 1870–1894

16 ***South Side of Harvard Square***
Location: Massachusetts Avenue,
Dunster Street to Holyoke Street
Date: 1870–1876
Photographer: Unknown
Source: Harvard University Archives

ॐ

During the 1870s Harvard Square was increasingly surrounded by buildings that combined a retail function at street level with student housing above. Private investment played a key role in this development. Of the eighteen dormitories built in the square between 1850 and 1900, only Holyoke House, shown here at left center, and College House were owned by Harvard College. The others were built by private investors.

Development of the block of Massachusetts Avenue between Dunster and Holyoke streets began in 1854 with the construction of Little's Block on the right, at the corner of Dunster Street. Charles C. Little built to the east of his first structure in 1869, and development was completed when Holyoke House filled in the remainder of the block in 1870.

Holyoke House was an imposing, four-and-a-half-story structure with luxurious facilities, including steam heat and a watercloset in each suite. Its grandeur was not outdone until the construction of the Gold Coast dormitories on Mount Auburn Street at the turn of the century.

It was the retail nature of these buildings that affected the daily lives of Cambridge residents. Lois Lilley Howe, in a paper for the Cambridge Historical Society, "Harvard Square in the 'Seventies and 'Eighties," describes these stores as "the most modern shops" at the time. For example, Francis H. Saunders, whose dry-goods store existed throughout the second half of the nineteenth century, was remembered for selling inexpensive Japanese products before they were common in this country.

This entire block was demolished in the early 1960s for the construction of Holyoke Center and Forbes Plaza.

17 *Memorial Hall*

Location: Cambridge and Kirkland streets
Date: c. 1888
Photographer: Percy Chase
Source: Harvard University Archives

Memorial Hall has been a major architectural focus of Harvard College and Cambridge for more than a century. This view from Cambridge Street shows the Harvard Civil War memorial prior to the numerous changes of the twentieth century.

Harvard began to make plans to erect a memorial to slain students and alumni in 1865, as the Civil War drew to a close. A Committee of Fifty was organized to see to the memorial's construction. The committee dictated that the building should contain a memorial hall, a banqueting hall, and a theater; they also urged the use of historical forms in the design.

Harvard held a competition for a suitable design, and in 1866 the committee selected the plan of Boston architects and Harvard alumni William Ware and Henry Van Brunt for a High Victorian Gothic-style structure. Two years later Ware and Van Brunt dramatically enlarged the design. The length of the memorial was increased from 132 to 310 feet. As requested, their plan for Memorial Hall included three distinct functional areas and was based on historical models. The alumni hall was patterned after Oxford and Cambridge dining halls, and Sanders Theatre after the Sheldonian Theatre at Oxford. The memorial hall itself, with plaques commemorating the dead, was centrally located under the tower.

Construction began in 1870 and was completed in 1878. The tower, which became a dominant feature of the Cambridge landscape, was embellished with additional pinnacles and elaborate cresting over the last four years of construction. In 1897 clocks were added to it. Gradually, in the twentieth century, much of Memorial Hall's ornamentation was removed, and a fire in 1956 destroyed the mansard roof of the tower.

At the left in this photograph is Daniel Chester French's statue of John Harvard, in its original position in front of Memorial Hall. The statue was dedicated on October 15, 1884; it was moved in 1924 to its present location in front of University Hall.

Percy Chase, the photographer, probably took this view prior to his graduation from Harvard in 1888. He was from Lynn, Massachusetts, and worked for several years as a naval architect in Boston after graduation. By 1894, Chase had gone into investment banking and remained in that business until his death, in 1914.

18 *Apthorp House*

Location: 15 Plympton Street
Date: c. 1880
Photographer: Unknown
Source: Society for the Preservation
of New England Antiquities

ა⋙

Once situated on a three-acre estate with terraced gardens and a view of the Charles River, the Apthorp House, built in 1760, is one of Cambridge's most important middle-Georgian-style residences.

Reverend East Apthorp, who built the house, was the son of a wealthy Boston merchant and the first rector of Christ Church. Christ Church was founded in Puritan Cambridge to serve the Anglican parish of Tory landowners and colonial officers who had recently built elaborate mansions on Brattle Street. Apthorp did not occupy the house, derisively known as the Bishop's Palace, for very long. In 1764 Apthorp emigrated to England and sold the house to John Borland, a Boston merchant who lived there until he died, in 1775. It was probably during Borland's ownership that the third story was added to the house. In 1803 Jonathan Simpson subdivided the property, and present-day Linden and Plympton streets were laid out on either side of the house.

In the late 1880s, as shown in this photograph, Apthorp House's Massachusetts Avenue frontage was still open, except for one house that had been built on the northeast corner of the block. In the left background are the towers of Gore Hall, Harvard's main library from 1838 until 1913.

Now totally hemmed in by later buildings, Apthorp House is surrounded to the north by the Harvard Squash Courts and to the east, south, and west by Randolph Hall of Harvard's Adams House. It is set in a U-shaped courtyard; a hint of its terraced gardens survives. Now the master's residence for Adams House, it has remained largely unaltered.

19 *Sturgis H. Thorndike*

Location: Unknown
Date: c. 1890
Photographer: James A. Wells
Source: Cambridge Historical Society

Sturgis H. Thorndike was an important designer of bridges for the city of Boston at the turn of the century. He was born in Beverly, Massachusetts, in 1868, but spent most of his life in Cambridge and Boston. In 1876 his family moved to Cambridge and bought a house at 22 Garden Street. After graduating from Harvard College in 1890 and receiving a degree in civil engineering from M.I.T. in 1895, Thorndike joined the Boston City Engineer's Department. Apart from a leave of absence from 1904 to 1906, when he was an instructor of civil engineering at M.I.T., Thorndike remained with the department until 1911. Thorndike designed the Charlestown, Summer Street, and Northern Avenue bridges in Boston and the Longfellow Bridge across the Charles River.

After several years of private practice following his departure from municipal service, Thorndike joined Frederic H. Fay and Charles M. Spofford to form the Boston engineering firm of Fay, Spofford & Thorndike; the firm still exists but is now located in Lexington.

A lifelong bachelor, Thorndike lived with his family on Garden Street for many years. Toward the end of his life he made his Lincoln summer home, Stony Farm, his legal residence. He was active in many civic, professional, and humanitarian organizations. One of his favorite avocations was mountain climbing; in particular, he enjoyed surveying and mapping the many trails of Mount Monadnock, in New Hampshire. Thorndike remained a participating partner in Fay, Spofford & Thorndike until his death in 1928.

James A. Wells, who took this photograph, was the first president of the Old Cambridge Photographic Club.

John the Orangeman

Location: Unknown
Date: c. 1890
Photographer: Unknown
Source: Cambridgeport Savings Bank

ટ્સ

This jovial man is John Lovett, "John the Orangeman," one of the best-loved figures on the Harvard campus in the last half of the nineteenth century.

John Lovett was born in County Kerry, Ireland, in 1833. Although his mother and two of his brothers came to this country while John was young, he did not follow his family until he was twenty.

Nicknamed for the fruit he peddled, John was a familiar sight on campus from 1855 until the turn of the century, with his cart of oranges and his donkey, Annie Radcliffe. An official mascot of the Harvard football and basketball teams—and listed that way in the city directories—John Lovett traveled with the teams to many New England colleges. He also attended Harvard Class Day and Commencement exercises for many years.

Although John Lovett boarded near Mason and Garden streets during his earliest years in Cambridge, by 1873 he had bought a house at 8 Beaver Street, where he lived until his death in 1906. Today Harvard's Mather House is located where John Lovett's house once stood.

21 *Cambridgeport Cycle Club*

Location: South side of Massachusetts
Avenue, east of Pearl Street
Date: c. 1890
Photographer: Unknown
Source: Cambridge Public Library

ဒ&

By the late 1800s, bicycling had become a popular pastime in the United
States. A Harvard cycle club that flourished between 1875 and 1890 took long
runs into the country, going as far
afield as Peterborough, New Hampshire. The Cambridgeport Cycle Club
was organized in February 1887. The
club met on the first and third Mon-
days of each month at 555 Main Street,
directly across the street from the location pictured.

The background of the photograph
shows something of the commercial
development of the Central Square
area in the late nineteenth century. The
commercial building behind the cy-
clists stood just west of the Odd Fel-
lows Hall; it was replaced in about
1910 by the brick building at 552–566
Massachusetts Avenue. At the center,
Freeman C. Witherell's fish market, established at that location around 1850
by Witherell's father, William, was the
structure's senior occupant. To the
right, Byron M. Snow's market,
opened in 1881, was a newer arrival to
the block; the other businesses were
more recent. George E. Shaw and
Austin S. Corey, who shared a nearby
house at 82 Green Street, ran Shaw &
Corey's Dining Rooms at the left,
serving "ladies and gents." Upstairs
were William E. Clarke, an architect
active in Cambridge in the 1890s, and
George E. Smith, whose tailor shop
opened in 1885.

22 *J. A. Holmes & Company*

Location: 636–638 Massachusetts
Avenue
Date: c. 1873
Photographer: Unknown
Source: Cambridgeport Savings Bank

ৈ

The J. A. Holmes & Company grocery store was one of Central Square's earliest businesses. J. A. Holmes, born in Cambridge in 1812, was working in the grocery business by the time he was eighteen years old as an employee of Edmund T. Hastings at 674 Massachusetts Avenue (then Main Street). Later Holmes became a partner in Hasting's grocery business.

In 1842 Holmes purchased "the old green store" pictured here, where he opened a family business that was a Central Square fixture well into the twentieth century. The building had been erected about 1800 and is seen here in one of its earliest forms. In later years it underwent several transformations, eventually becoming hidden behind a multistory brick exterior. Parts of both the old frame building and the later brick exterior may still exist behind the current two-story facade.

J. A. Holmes lived at 55 Magazine Street, not far from his business. Known as Deacon Holmes because of his association with the First Baptist Church, visible at the right in this photograph, he also served as city councilor, city treasurer, and president of the Cambridgeport Savings Bank.

23   *Civil War Veterans*
Location: Unknown
Date: c. 1886
Photographer: Unknown
Source: William Conway

ॐ

Assembled here are the survivors of the first company raised in the United States for the suppression of the Rebellion, Company C, Third Regiment, Massachusetts Volunteer Militia, which left Cambridge on April 16, 1861.

The company was the result of the efforts of James P. Richardson, a Cambridge attorney who, anticipating the coming war, urged Cambridge residents to enlist in defense of the Union.

The sixty men who responded to his appeal were later joined by thirty-seven more; altogether, they constituted the first organized company of militia in the United States enlisted specifically for the defense of the government in the Rebellion of 1861. The militia, under the command of Richardson, represented a variety of Cambridge professions, including a printer, a bacon curer, a confectioner, a clerk, a teamster, and many city firemen. The members of this Massachusetts militia were referred to as the Cambridge City Guard. The men had enlisted for three months, but all except two reenlisted. Twenty-one died in battle.

The survivors of the First Company met annually after the war, and the company celebrated its twenty-fifth anniversary in 1886; it is likely that this photograph was taken on that occasion. In the same year, the company marched in a parade with other veterans, accompanied by their drummer, Charlie Copp, who carried the same drum he had carried during the Civil War.

24 *Cambridge Electric Company Workers*

Location: Albro Street(?)
Date: 1888
Photographer: Unknown
Source: Cambridge Electric Light Company

The Cambridge Electric Light Company first supplied electricity in 1886 from a small electric generating plant in the Kendall Square area near the West Boston Bridge. This plant was installed to service the electric arc lights that had just been erected along Main Street from the West Boston Bridge to Brattle Square. The city's streets had previously been illuminated by gas. The city's increased demands for electrical power made the Kendall Square plant inadequate within a few years. Although some businesses had power plants of their own, most of the electrical power necessary for the rapidly growing city was supplied by Cambridge Electric Light Company.

In 1888 land was purchased on Western Avenue near the Charles River for the construction of the new power plant seen here. The river site was important because coal for the boilers that powered the generators could be brought up the river directly to the plant.

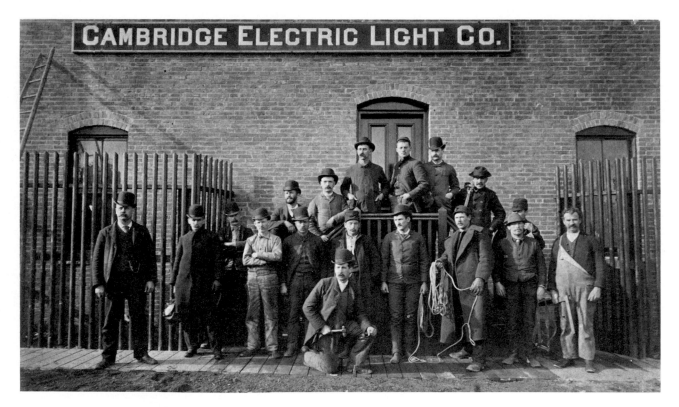

25 *Palmer Street Saloon*

Location: One Palmer Street
Date: c. 1880
Photographer: Unknown
Source: Marie Costello

ॐ

Daniel Clark, standing under the sign, was the owner of this Harvard Square saloon from 1881 until 1886. The group of gentlemen accompanying him are probably patrons, some of whom might have assembled from nearby businesses such as the carriage shops on Palmer and Church streets.

When a local ordinance restricting the public sale of liquor was passed in 1886, Daniel Clark was forced to close his saloon. The liquor license issue had been hotly debated for a number of years. Several groups, such as the No-License Committee of Cambridge, the Home Protection League, and the Law and Order League, had made persistent yearly efforts since 1881 to outlaw saloons. After his saloon was closed, Daniel Clark went to work in Boston as a bartender and waiter. He later operated a lodging house at his home at 10 Eliot Street.

According to a member of Daniel Clark's family, Daniel never touched a drop of liquor until the day he died, when a well-intentioned individual tried to revive him by giving him a shot of whiskey.

26 *George O. Rollins Carriage Shop*

Location: 23-25 Church Street
Date: 1873–1893
Photographer: Unknown
Source: Marion Colby

ૐ

George O. Rollins owned and ran a carriage shop from approximately 1873 to 1893. The Church and Palmer Street area was a center of the Cambridge carriage business, including among its establishments carriage builders, blacksmiths, and livery stable owners, as well as painters and carpenters.

Born in 1836, Rollins was engaged in the carriage business by 1866 and owned his Church Street business by 1873. In 1893 he and George M. Church became successors to the Chapman Carriage Company of 13-15 Brattle Street, well known for its Chapman, Goddard, and Stanhope buggies. However, by the year of his death, in 1901, George O. Rollins had gone back into business for himself on Palmer Street.

In his earliest years as a carriage builder, George O. Rollins lived at Chapman Place. From 1891 until his death in 1901 he lived at 22 Farwell Place, not far from where he worked.

The only reminder of the once extensive wagon and blacksmith trade in Harvard Square is the brick building on Church Street at the head of Palmer Street. Built in 1864 as a police station, 31-33 Church Street was sold by the city in 1874 and became the carriage shop of James White, whose painted sign is still visible in the gable.

27 *Hugh and William McCaffrey, Harness Makers*

Location: 945 Cambridge Street
Date: 1891
Photographer: Garth & Williams, Boston
Source: Margaret McCaffrey

ॐ

Hugh McCaffrey's harness shop featured a wide variety of items, from a "good calf skin razor strap for 25¢" to "axle grease, slightly damaged, for 4¢ a box," all at "less than Boston prices." William Henry McCaffrey, the son of Hugh McCaffrey, stands in front of the family business in this photograph.

Hugh McCaffrey, born in 1829, came to the United States from County Tyrone in northern Ireland in the 1840s. He became an American citizen in 1852. McCaffrey opened a business on Charlestown Street in Boston but in about 1880 moved to Cambridge and established himself as a saddler and harness maker. He prospered in this trade and at one time owned three shops—one on Boylston Street and one in East Cambridge, as well as the Cambridge Street shop.

Hugh McCaffrey and his family lived at 197 Hampshire Street in Cambridge from the 1880s until 1901, when they moved to 123 Inman Street. McCaffrey lived there until his death in 1903, when his son William took over the family business.

F. X. Massé Store

Location: 256 Walden Street, corner of
Sherman Street
Date: 1894
Photographer: Unknown
Source: Massé Hardware

This photograph is one of many documenting the Massé family business. The owner, Francis X. Massé, is standing at the right, with his son Ernest seated in front of him. With the storeowner are, at the left, John McAdoo, a teamster, and next to him, Pat Curley, a local contractor. The identity of the man in the doorway is not known.

Francis X. Massé came to this country from Rivière Ouelle, Quebec, in 1881. He worked as a baker in Cambridge before opening his general store in 1888 at 256 Walden Street, on the ground floor of a residence that still stands. At the time of this photograph, the store faced the vast brickyard complex of the Bay State Brick Company across Walden Street. By 1899 Mr. Massé's business had prospered, and he moved business and family diagonally across Walden Street. During the First World War, Massé found it difficult to hire help and closed his general store. He replaced it with a hardware business at the same location, which the Massé family continues today.

29 *The Rand Estate*
(Exterior and Interior)

Location: 112 Elm Street
Date: c. 1890
Photographer: Unknown
Source: Cambridge Historical Society

The Rand estate on Elm Street in North Cambridge dated back to at least 1850, when Benjamin Rand acquired the large property. In 1859 Henry C. Rand inherited the property, which then comprised nearly an acre of land extending from Massachusetts Avenue to Elm Street. There were two main residences, as well as a barn, a greenhouse, an orchard, and extensive gardens. Henry C. Rand worked in the leather business in Boston at 45 Merchants Row during the 1880s and 1890s. His son, Harry S. Rand, joined him in the business in 1882. The estate survived until 1952, when the land was cleared for the Porter Square Shopping Center.

Jean Tewksbury Rand is shown in October 1892 entertaining a guest from New York City, Rebecca Caldwell, in her home on the Rand estate. The fashionably dressed ladies are having tea; the intimate interior scene vividly conveys the feeling of a well-appointed late-nineteenth-century parlor.

**Curtis Davis Sleigh and
George Page Box Company**
Location: Hampshire Street at
Broadway
Date: 1889
Photographer: Unknown
Source: Curtis Mellen

Two of the most important industries of nineteenth- and early-twentieth-century Cambridge are represented in this photograph. The horse-drawn sleigh is carrying crates of soap manufactured by Curtis Davis & Company, whose plant became the first Lever Brothers factory in the U.S. In the background stands the George G. Page Box Company, said to have been the largest box manufacturer in New England during the late nineteenth century.

Curtis Davis established his soap business in 1835. Three years later he entered a partnership with Alexander Dickinson. The firm operated as Davis & Dickinson for many years. When the partnership dissolved in 1851, Davis acquired property at Broadway and Portland Street for Curtis Davis & Company.

In 1883 Curtis Davis & Company developed an innovative marketing strategy. Abandoning their practice of manufacturing more than 125 brands of soap, the firm limited production to fewer than six brands, but advertised their Welcome brand of soap widely, using a handshake as their trademark.

This venture proved successful, and the company continued to grow throughout the late nineteenth century; it was taken over by Lever Brothers at the turn of the century. Lever Brothers maintained the Welcome trademark and, until the end of the 1950s, occupied a huge factory complex on the block bounded by Broadway, Portland, Washington, and Burleigh streets, now the site of the George Stark Draper Laboratory near Technology Square.

The George G. Page Box Company had its beginnings in 1844, when New Hampshire native George Page settled in Cambridge and began manufacturing boxes and packing cases. From its early years as a tiny operation with one horse and two or three employees, Page's business grew until, by the 1850s, the firm employed nearly 100 workers using machinery powered by a thirty-horsepower engine. A major part of the company's business was the manufacture of cigar boxes.

The brick building shown here is Page's Factory No. 1, built in 1874 on the site of two earlier Page buildings destroyed by fire. Lumber was delivered to the first floor of this building, at first only from Page's mills in Maine but later, as the business expanded, including the entire output of five mills in Maine and Massachusetts. Rollers slid the lumber directly into planing machines. From there the planed wood went to saws that cut the proper lengths and widths for the various boxes. A matching machine joined the pieces to form the boxes. Finally, the printing department, located on the second floor, printed brand names directly on the wood—an 1876 innovation by George Page that saved the expense of printing and pasting labels.

The George G. Page Box Company continued to grow through the last quarter of the nineteenth century, but declined in the twentieth century. By 1929 Page's was no longer in business, and the property belonged to the Boston Woven Hose & Rubber Company, the longtime occupant of the site next door. Factory No. 1, shown here, was demolished in December 1982.

III 1895–1914

32 *Harvard Square on Class Day*

Location: Massachusetts Avenue at Holyoke Street, looking east
Date: c. 1905
Photographer: Detroit Publishing Company
Source: Library of Congress

ॐ

The buildings in this view of Harvard Square may look much the same as they did in the 1870s, but the end of the century had brought dramatic changes. When the West End Street Railway converted its horsecar routes through Cambridge to electric traction in 1889, the effects were far-reaching. The new trolleys cut the travel time from Cambridge to Boston to a fraction of that needed by the horsecars, increasing Cambridge's appeal as a convenient residential area for Boston commuters. As Harvard Square became a major transportation center at the turn of the century, commerce flourished. By the time of this view, the street at this busy intersection had been paved for the first time.

The increased activity, compounded by the tremendous noise of the new streetcars, caused Harvard College to shift its focus away from the square. Historically, Harvard's orientation had been toward the square, its early quadrangles all open to the street. No major visual barrier intervened between college and town throughout the nineteenth century, for the fence surrounding the Yard was composed merely of granite posts supporting three wooden rails. However, the bustle of the late-nineteenth-century square, coincident with Harvard's transformation to a university of national standing, led the administration to seek a physical separation of the institution from the town.

During Charles W. Eliot's presidency (1869–1909), the student population rose from 1,060 to 3,692, necessitating a large building program. The new dormitories built in Harvard Yard—Thayer, Weld, and Matthews halls—focused greater attention on the center of the Yard. Most decisive in

separating the college from the square was the 1901 erection of the Memorial Fence. Designed by McKim, Mead and White, the brick-and-wrought-iron fence, seen to the far right in the photograph, is pierced by nine major gates and several minor ones.

This photograph was taken on Harvard's Class Day, an occasion of festivities for the senior class on commencement.

Subway Construction in Harvard Square

Location: Harvard Square from Palmer Street
Date: 1910
Photographer: Boston Elevated Railway
Source: Cambridge Historical Commission

ᏅᎦ

Only four years after the preceding photograph, Harvard Square was turned on its head by the construction of the subway from Boston. Proposals to improve travel between Harvard Square and Boston had been discussed for many years, and the proponents of a steam-powered elevated railroad traveling over Massachusetts Avenue and Main Street had nearly succeeded in the 1880s. Instead, the Boston Elevated Railway won legislative permission to construct a subway and began work in 1909. Planning had actually begun several years before; when the Longfellow Bridge was constructed between 1900 and 1906 it included a fenced, double track right-of-way as well as streetcar tracks in the roadway.

The impact of subway construction on Harvard Square was considerable, although probably less than during the construction of the Alewife extension from 1979 to 1985. Massachusetts Avenue was widened, eliminating the front yard of Wadsworth House, shown here in the center background. Then the subway trench was excavated, decked over with planking, and lined with concrete while traffic passed overhead. The same techniques were used in the more recent project, although the planners did not have to maintain trolley service. Construction was completed in 1912 some months ahead of schedule, in part because of the innovative use of electric motors rather than steam engines in construction. If conventional techniques had been used, the derrick in the right foreground would have been powered by steam, with inevitable heavy pollution. Once the subway was completed, the office building at Four Brattle Street was constructed on the vacant lot next to the old Lyceum Hall, and Harvard Square assumed the appearance it would maintain for the next seventy years.

34 *Central Square Looking South*

Location: Junction of Massachusetts
Avenue, Magazine Street, River Street,
and Western Avenue
Date: 1910–1913
Photographer: Unknown
Source: Society for the Preservation of
New England Antiquities

ঽ✒

In this view of Central Square the diverse elements—commercial, religious, and social—that have traditionally been represented there converge.

The First Baptist Church, in the center, at the junction of Magazine and River streets, was a visual focus for Central Square throughout most of the nineteenth century. Shown here is the 1881 structure designed by Hartwell & Richardson, which still stands.

Flanking the church and forming a triangle with Massachusetts Avenue are a pair of mansard-roofed commercial buildings. The wooden structure to the right dates from the early nineteenth century. Its appearance and function changed many times over the years. The Cambridge YMCA operated there from 1885 to 1897, when the organization moved to its present location across from City Hall.

In this postcard view, Central Square was given an air of modernity with a pasted-in image of an automobile. The Cambridge Theatre, in the distance to the right of the First Baptist Church, was showing vaudeville productions, but would soon convert to a moving-picture theater.

35 *The Cambridge Theatre*

Location: 22 Western Avenue
Date: 1912
Photographer: Unknown
Source: G. Campbell

ॐ

The Cambridge Theatre stood at the junction of Western Avenue and River Street from 1910 until its demolition in 1954. Designed by Cambridge architect Charles R. Greco, this unusual theater was built for vaudeville productions. The shows usually ran for one week, with tickets ranging from fifteen to fifty cents. Prominently advertised in the *Cambridge Chronicle,* they had such titles as *Merely Mary Ann, Paid in Full, Quincy Adams Sawyer,* and *Her Son,* which was billed as "one of the strongest plays of the year."

On January 27, 1913, the theater reopened as the Olympia Theatre, following renovations that probably brought moving pictures there for the first time. According to the *Chronicle's* enthusiastic report the following week, the Olympia was packed for every performance. The report adds, "The patronage and support advanced by the public show the interest in the newest form of entertainment, and it seems assured that feature photo-plays have come to stay."

In 1954 the structure was replaced by a gas station.

36 *Coffee Counter*

Location: J. A. Holmes & Company,
638 Massachusetts Avenue
Date: 1904–1910
Photographer: Unknown
Source: Cambridgeport Savings Bank

ۋ

This photograph of the coffee counter
at the front of the J. A. Holmes grocery store (next door to the Central
Square Market in the following photograph) gives a unique interior and exterior view of early-twentieth-century
Central Square. The two men in derby
hats are taking advantage of the offer
of hot coffee for two and four cents a
cup. Through the window three major
structures along Massachusetts Avenue
display the architectural diversity of
Central Square. At the left, behind the
woman serving coffee, stands the
early-nineteenth-century wooden frame
building remodeled for the Cambridge
YMCA in 1885. This simple structure
contrasts with the towered Roman-
esque Cambridge City Hall across
Massachusetts Avenue, designed and
built by Longfellow, Alden & Harlow
in 1888. At the extreme right is the
Renaissance-inspired 1904 Cambridgeport Savings Bank designed by
Chamberlin & Blackall.

37 *Central Square Market—J. A. Holmes & Company*

Location: 1–5 Central Square
Date: c. 1900
Photographer: Unknown
Source: Cambridgeport Savings Bank

꒰ଽ

The J. A. Holmes & Company grocery business had enjoyed prosperity and considerable growth since its inception in 1842, in the congenial commercial atmosphere of late-nineteenth-century Central Square.

The original Holmes store featured West India goods, such as rum and molasses, and bulk items. By the time of this photograph the family business was in its second generation. Joseph A. Holmes, the founder, had died in 1893, and his son, Francis M. Holmes, presided over a complex of adjacent stores. The original frame Holmes building at 636–638 Massachusetts Avenue was now hidden behind a three-story mansard brick structure and was combined with an adjoining building very similar in style, just visible to the left. In addition, the Holmes family had acquired the Nay & Dodge Market, pictured here, where fresh fruits, vegetables, and meats were sold. To the right is the Central Square Market delivery wagon, still drawn by horse.

Francis Marshall Holmes had first worked as a clerk in the Boston grocery business of Henry Callender & Company, and then worked in the flour business before taking over the family grocery store. Like his father, Francis was active in the First Baptist Church and lived on Magazine Street, the street where he grew up, not far from the J. A. Holmes grocery stores.

**Dr. Albert Lowe Norris House
(Exterior and Interior)**
Location: 760 Massachusetts Avenue
Date: c. 1900
Photographer: Dr. Albert P. Norris(?)
Source: Cambridgeport Savings Bank

℘

Dr. Albert Lowe Norris was a well-
known Cambridge physician of the
nineteenth century. He was born in
Epping, New Hampshire, in 1839,
studied at Exeter Academy and Harvard Medical School, and took post-
graduate courses in Vienna, Berlin, and
Edinburgh. He began practicing
medicine in Cambridge in 1862, but almost immediately left for three years'
service in the Union Army. His earliest home and office were located on
Cambridge Street in East Cambridge,
but by 1880 Dr. Norris and his family
had moved to this house near Central
Square.

During the nineteenth century this section of Massachusetts Avenue was primarily residential, in contrast to the commercial atmosphere dominant today. Dr. Norris's home was located on the corner of Pleasant Street adjacent to the Athenaeum building that then served as City Hall. In 1888 the new City Hall replaced a house across the street, and in 1933 Dr. Norris's house was torn down and replaced by the main post office.

The photograph of the house was probably taken on a Fourth of July at the turn of the century. Both photographs may well have been taken by Dr. Norris's son, Dr. Albert P. Norris, an amateur photographer and, like his father, a physician.

39 *Inman Square*

Location: Intersection of Hampshire and Cambridge streets, looking east
Date: c. 1895
Photographer: Unknown
Source: Society for the Preservation of New England Antiquities

Inman Square was named for Ralph Inman, a Tory merchant whose Mid Cambridge estate extended from Massachusetts Avenue to the Somerville line. This view shows both electric trolleys and horse-drawn carts, as well as two significant structures still associated with Inman Square.

The three-story brick building at the far left was constructed in 1874, and housed at different times the Inman Trust Company, Lechmere National Bank, and Middlesex Bank. Today the ground floor houses a grocery store, while the upper floors have been converted from a dance hall to offices.

The former Inman Square Hotel dominates the center of the photograph. Built for Charles Waite as a house and store in 1855, this three-story Greek Revival structure is one of Cambridge's most impressive surviving nineteenth-century commercial buildings. It was converted to apartments and the ground floor made into a grocery store in 1888. In 1916 the yellow brick Waite Building, designed by Newhall & Blevins, was joined to it. In 1983 the yellow paint first applied in 1916 was removed in a partial restoration.

Behind the block of one-story buildings at the right is the Inman Square firehouse tower, which was used for drying fire hoses. The firehouse was designed in 1874 by James Fogerty, an architect-builder responsible for a variety of Cambridge buildings, including other firehouses, schools, factories, and many residences. The Inman Square firehouse was replaced in 1912 by the present firehouse designed by Newhall & Blevins.

The West End Street Railway trolley cars seen here linked parts of Cambridge with Boston and Somerville. The car approaching the camera was coming from North Station in Boston toward Harvard Square; the other car was on a route to Spring Hill via Union Square in Somerville.

40 *Cambridge Street Houses*

Location: 192–218 Cambridge Street
Date: 1893–1895
Photographer: Unknown
Source: Middlesex County

Cambridge Street was completed in 1809 to provide a continuous route from Old Cambridge to Boston via Craigie's Bridge, which stood at the site of the present Charles River Dam. By 1862 the street had become East Cambridge's major public transportation artery as the route of a horsecar line from Harvard Square to Boston. The tracks of the horsecar line are visible in the lower right-hand corner of this photograph.

At the left is part of a double house built at 192–194 Cambridge Street in 1828 by John L. Hobbs, a glass cutter at the New England Glass Company. A gifted craftsman, Hobbs had advanced rapidly and became superintendent of the company's cutting department in 1825, at the age of twenty-one. The simple double house had a frame construction, but a heavy brick partition separated the two halves, providing fire protection. In the year the house was constructed, Hobbs sold half of it to Ephraim Buttrick, an attorney. Buttrick lived there until 1849, convenient both to the Middlesex County Courthouse and downtown Boston. Hobbs later left East Cambridge to found his own glass company in West Virginia.

More substantial than Hobbs's structure were the three-story brick houses seen in the center. As early as 1810 the Lechmere Point Corporation, the developer of East Cambridge, required that all large structures built within twenty feet of the street be constructed of brick or stone. These two brick houses at 196–210 Cambridge Street provide an example of the sort of substantial buildings the corporation hoped to encourage. Built about 1825, the houses were sold in 1827 to Samuel Parker of Charlestown. Parker turned the east half over to his daughter when she married Dr. Anson Hooker, a prominent East Cambridge physician. Parker and the Hookers lived here until their deaths, around 1870.

At midcentury, this stretch of Cambridge Street between Second and Third streets was a residential area, inhabited by attorneys, merchants, and physicians; farther west a number of commercial buildings were mixed with existing residences. By the time of this late-century photograph, this block also had become increasingly commercial, containing all three of East Cambridge's banks. One of these, the East Cambridge Savings Bank, is visible here at 204 Cambridge Street, in the former Parker–Hooker House. The bank had purchased the building from Dr. Anson Hooker's heirs in 1873; it remained in this storefront location until 1895. In that year, Middlesex County purchased all the buildings shown here and demolished them to make room for the new Registry of Deeds, which now occupies the entire block between Cambridge, Otis, Second, and Third streets.

41 *Third District Court*

Location: City Building Courtroom,
Eliot Square
Date: 1905
Photographer: Unknown
Source: Paul Beecher, Third District
Court

ॐ

The Third District Court of Eastern Middlesex County was established in 1882, with jurisdiction over Cambridge, Arlington, and Belmont. Shown here is the interior of the City Building courtroom at 110 Mt. Auburn Street.

The first sessions of the police court, the predecessor of the present district court, were held in East Cambridge in 1859. Later the court was located in the police headquarters at 31-33 Church Street. By 1875, the court had moved to the City Building in Eliot Square. The City Building housed not only the police court and then the district court, but also a police station, engine house, ward meeting room, and city offices. The structure was demolished in 1935.

In 1913, the district court moved to a building in the county jail complex in East Cambridge, and stayed there until 1931, when a courthouse was built on Third Street. It is now located in the new courthouse.

Emerson W. Law, at the far right, was the first clerk of the district court, having previously been clerk of the police court. Frank A. Hagar, at the far left, was the son of Frank W. Hagar, a probation officer in the earlier police court.

42 *Counting Room, The Riverside Press*

Location: Memorial Drive at River Street
Date: 1896–1905
Photographer: Unknown
Source: Cambridge Historical Commission collection

࠹

The Riverside Press was founded in 1852 by Henry O. Houghton. Born in Vermont in 1823, Houghton graduated from the University of Vermont in 1846 and joined the Cambridge printing firm of Freeman & Bolles. The firm, which printed law books for Boston publisher Little, Brown & Co., soon offered him a partnership. Little, Brown was sufficiently pleased with the firm's work that they purchased for them the old Cambridge almshouse on the Charles River at River Street. Now doing business as H. O. Houghton & Co., the company prospered, more than doubling its facilities in 1867 and establishing a lithography department in 1875. The firm became Houghton, Mifflin & Co. in 1880, and at the end of the century was famous for its Riverside Editions of the classics, designed by the artist Bruce Shaw. Houghton, Mifflin operated the Riverside Press at its original location until 1971, when the plant was closed and the buildings demolished. The site is now the Riverside Press Park.

Houghton also served as mayor of Cambridge, and lived in an elegant house on Massachusetts Avenue near Dana Street. His business sense and attention to detail were well known, as was his memory for dereliction. He was responsible for the firm's motto: *Tout bien ou rien*—Do it well or not at all. That Houghton dominated his company is evident in this photograph of the counting room, where his portrait hung flanked by curtains that were presumably drawn at night. Probably taken after Houghton's death in 1895, the photograph shows a modern office with a communications system of speaking tubes on the column in the foreground.

43 ***Noon Class at***
John P. Squire & Company
Location: 165 Gore Street
Date: c. 1900
Photographer: Unknown
Source: Cambridge YMCA

The Cambridge YMCA sponsored
noon classes in English for the
thousands of newly arrived immigrants
working in Cambridge businesses, in
this case at J. P. Squire & Company.
Lunch-hour classes were held not only
at Squire's, but also at other major city
industries, including Boston Woven
Hose and Rubber Company, National
Casket Company, and Blake Manufacturing Company. The classes were often taught by Harvard undergraduates.

John P. Squire & Company, a pork-
processing business, was located on the
Miller's River in East Cambridge. One
of the city's largest industries, its prop-
erties filled a two-block area of reclaimed land north of Gore Street. By
1896, Squire's employed at least 1,000
men and women and was ranked as
the third-largest company of its kind in
the United States.

44 *Lawrence Dairy Wagon*
Location: 2307-2309 Massachusetts
Avenue
Date: c. 1907
Photographer: Unknown
Source: Mrs. Julia Griffin

&

The Lawrence Dairy Farm in Lexington, Massachusetts was purchased in
1907 by the Griffin brothers, who had
come from County Cork, Ireland, to
Cambridge. At one time there were
three brothers active in the family
dairy business, John, Patrick, and
Bartholomew. This photograph shows
John and Pat Griffin with their milk-
delivery wagon, outside their home on
Massachusetts Avenue. The milk was
probably brought by train to the
North Cambridge station from the
Lexington dairy, then bottled in a barn
behind the family house. The Griffins
continued the dairy business until
1946. John Griffin, head of the firm at
that time, then started a funeral business, which continues at the same location on Massachusetts Avenue.

45 *Manual Training School Fire Brigade*

Location: Manual Training School, between Broadway and Cambridge Street
Date: c. 1895
Photographer: N. L. Stebbins
Source: Marion Colby

ૐ➤

The Manual Training School was one of a number of public buildings constructed in Cambridge as a result of the philanthropy of Frederick Hastings Rindge. Rindge was born in Cambridge in 1857, and on the death of his mother in 1885, he inherited $3 million. He then married and moved to California, where he purchased the Spanish land grant now occupied by Santa Monica and Malibu. The gifts to Cambridge, to which Rindge only returned for visits, included the Manual Training School and Library in 1889, Cambridge City Hall in 1889, and the Harvard Epworth Methodist Church in 1891. The school was demolished in 1931 and replaced by the present Cambridge High School.

The Manual Training School offered classes in fire-fighting techniques, and in this photograph the student fire-brigade ladder truck and crew pose in front of the school. There were several hose companies in the fire-fighting program; larger boys were assigned to the ladder company. Between 1891 and 1894 the school's fire department added the ladder truck shown here, which was either drawn by hand or pulled by horses. The school also acquired a hose wagon, used only with horses, and a drill tower, The horse-drawn equipment was added so that officers from the school could assist local firemen during a general-alarm fire.

William M. Colby, in the driver's seat of the student brigade wagon, had run a furniture-moving business in Boston, and in 1891 he and his brother Horace opened a moving business in the Lyceum Building in Harvard Square. The Colby brothers received orders by mail or messenger and had five teams of horses ready to make deliveries or to assist fire-fighting units such as this one at the school. They also advertised a barge for parties that would hold twenty passengers.

N. L. Stebbins, the photographer, was also in the furniture business in Boston between 1880 and 1884. He became a commercial photographer on Washington Street in Boston in 1884; he was later known nationally for his photographs of marine subjects.

46 *J. Bouchard Provisions*

Location: 86–88 Harvey Street, corner of Montgomery Street
Date: c. 1910
Photographer: Unknown
Source: Emily Broussard

Many French Canadians came to Cambridge between 1890 and 1900 to work in brickyards and factories. Jean Bouchard, shown second from the left in this photograph of his family home and grocery store, came from Quebec. He started his grocery business in 1910 in the northwest part of the city, where many French Canadian families lived at that time, not far from the Notre Dame de Pitie Church at the corner of Harvey and Westley streets.

Bouchard was assisted in his business by members of the de Patie family, as well as by his own family. Both Augustin de Patie, at Bouchard's left, and his brother Armand, at Bouchard's right, worked at the grocery for a number of years. The de Patie brothers grew up in Cambridge; their parents had come from Nova Scotia and Quebec. Bouchard and his family lived above their grocery in a house built in 1886 and still standing.

Mr. and Mrs. George W. Lewis

Location: 47 Parker Street
Date: c. 1900
Photographer: Unknown
Source: Roberta Hankamer

ર્≈

George Washington Lewis was steward of Harvard's exclusive Porcellian Club for forty-five years and then steward emeritus until he died.

Born in Cambridge in 1848, Lewis worked with his father, also George W. Lewis, who was steward before him, for several years before replacing his father in 1876. Lewis was renowned for his intelligence and exceptional memory and was one of the best-loved members of the Harvard community.

The Lewis family bought the house at 47 Parker Street in 1897. This structure was home for black undergraduates at Harvard and was the setting for many family and student activities, including a number of amateur theatricals.

When George W. Lewis died at eighty-one, in 1929, the service at Christ Church included the boys' choir (of which Lewis had once been a member) singing many of Lewis's favorite hymns, and some of Harvard's most distinguished graduates, such as Theodore Lyman (class of 1897) and Henry B. Cabot Jr. (class of 1917), as pallbearers.

48 **John B. Frongillo**

Location: Studio portrait
Date: c. 1910
Photographer: Oppenheim Studio,
Boston
Source: Charles M. Sullivan

John B. Frongillo, a cabinetmaker by trade, was born Giovanni Frongillo in Avellino, Italy, in 1884. Little is known of his early years, but Avellino, which is both a city and a province of Campania, an agricultural region in the hinterland of Naples, was the source of thousands of immigrants to the United States at the turn of the century. Taxation in the period bore especially hard on Italian peasants and small farmers, and parts of the country were among the most densely populated in Europe.

When Frongillo arrived in the North End of Boston at the turn of the century, he found a community of 28,000, predominately Italian but with large numbers of Russian Jews and a strong rear guard of the Irish, who had originally displaced the Yankees in the 1840s. In the 1880s there were barely a thousand Italians in the North End, but by 1895 this had increased to 7,700. Already the neighborhood had become the main receiving area for Italian immigrants to Boston, many of whom settled in the North End before moving on to Italian neighborhoods in other communities.

In 1927, Frongillo purchased an 1850s house at 37 Cogswell Avenue in the predominately Irish community of North Cambridge. Perhaps attracted there by his relatives the Struzzieros, who lived next door, John and his wife Clementina remodeled their house and began to cultivate wine grapes and vegetables. A skilled wood-carver and chairmaker, he established a cabinetmaking shop in the old stable and carried on a trade in custom furniture.

Frongillo also worked for many years at the Irving & Casson–A. H. Davenport Company. This East Cambridge company was known for its fine furniture and architectural woodwork, filling commissions for such architects as H. H. Richardson, Ralph Adams Cram, and McKim, Mead & White. Among the projects Frongillo worked on was the reredos of St. Patrick's Cathedral in New York. Many of the chairs he made privately in his North Cambridge shop were copied from Irving & Casson designs.

Frongillo prospered in North Cambridge, and by the time of his second marriage in 1943 to Antoinetta Piazzola he owned lots in Chelsea, Everett, and Somerville. He lived in the house on Cogswell Avenue until he died in 1973.

50 *Edwin Davis Mellen House*

Location: 1590 Massachusetts Avenue
Date: c. 1899
Photographer: Edwin D. Mellen(?)
Source: Curtis Mellen

In 1896, Edwin Davis Mellen, then owner of the Curtis Davis Soap Company, commissioned the Boston architectural firm of Hartwell, Richardson & Driver to design this large Colonial Revival house on Massachusetts Avenue, just north of Cambridge Common. The earlier firm of Hartwell & Richardson had designed a Shingle Style house at 33 Washington Avenue for Edwin Mellen's father, James, in 1887. Both Washington Avenue and this part of Massachusetts Avenue (then called North Avenue) were fashionable new addresses at the time. However, the popularity of North Avenue declined with the arrival of the noisy electric streetcars in the 1890s.

Edwin Mellen was the grandson of Curtis Davis, founder of the family soap business. The company was still under the management of Davis and his son-in-law James Mellen in 1882, when Edwin Mellen completed his studies at M.I.T. and joined the business. Edwin served as chemist and superintendent until Curtis Davis's death in February 1887, when he was made a partner. In 1896, Edwin's father, James, died, and Stillman F. Kelley, owner of a large sugar and molasses business, became Edwin Mellen's partner.

Mellen remained with the family business until about 1906, several years after Lever Brothers had bought a controlling interest. He continued to live in the house on Massachusetts Avenue until 1916, when he and his wife, Adele, moved to an apartment building at 44 Langdon Street. The house eventually became a rooming house known as The Greycroft. It was demolished in 1980.

This photograph may have been taken by Edwin Mellen himself. Mellen was an active amateur photographer who left an invaluable collection from the 1880s through the early 1900s.

51 *Charles River Basin Seawall*

Location: Charles River Basin, near
Massachusetts Avenue, looking
northeast
Date: 1897
Photographer: Unknown
Source: Cambridge Park Department
Annual Report, 1897

ॐ

The end of the nineteenth century
brought major changes in the appearance of Cambridge. One of these was
the construction of the granite Charles
River Basin seawall, which eventually
ran from Longfellow Bridge upstream
to a point halfway between the Harvard and the Boston University
bridges. By the completion of the seawall in the early 1900s, the Cambridge
riverfront was transformed from foul-
smelling marshes and mud flats to
more than 200 acres of usable land
along a river basin no longer dramatically affected by the tides.

The plan proposed by the Charles
River Embankment Company in 1881
called for the development of a fashionable residential area on the newly
filled land. The granite seawall was begun in 1883, and a design for the residential area and ornamental esplanade
was prepared in 1889 by Frederick
Viaux. Considerable progress was
made in reclaiming land, filling it with
mud dredged from the river side of the
new wall.

In 1893, the Charles River Embankment Company collapsed, but by 1896
the Cambridge Park Commission took
up the work of completing the project.
Although the plans for residential development never materialized, the esplanade was completed.

The Massachusetts Institute of Technology was built to the left of the portion of the riverfront in this view. In
the background are several buildings
behind Main Street near Kendall
Square.

52 *Magazine Beach*

Location: South end of Magazine Street
Date: 1906
Photographer: Unknown
Source: Walter L. Colburn

Magazine Beach was a popular Cambridge riverfront park from its creation at the turn of the century. The beach and street were named for a state powder magazine, built there in 1818. The location was also known as Captain's Island, after Captain Daniel Patrick, said to have been Dutch, who from 1632 to 1637 owned five acres surrounding a small hillock rising from the salt marsh.

The Cambridge Park Department made plans to develop Magazine Beach in the 1890s as part of a massive program of land filling, park construction, and development of the riverfront. Olmsted Brothers, the Boston landscape-architecture firm that succeeded Frederick Law Olmsted's firm, was commissioned by the City of Cambridge for a number of park projects, including work at Magazine Beach. The former magazine building on the site was in ruins; Olmsted Brothers used its stone blocks to construct a locker house, which still stands. The beach itself was made partly with gravel from the knoll on Captain's Island, but primarily with sand dredged from the river. The appeal of the beach was apparently not diminished by the Beacon Park yard of the Boston & Albany Railroad across the river in Allston.

Magazine Beach quickly became a major center of summer activity. According to the Cambridge Annual Report of 1899, the beach was patroled by "two life savers in swimming apparel and a park police officer." The current in this section of the river was strong, so life lines enclosed the swimming area. In 1900 the Annual Report estimated that 25,000 people had used the beach that summer. Swimming at Magazine Beach remained popular until after World War II, when pollution of the Charles River necessitated construction of a swimming pool at the adjacent park.

53 *Harvard Square*

Location: Harvard Square, looking
southwest from Massachusetts Avenue
Date: c. 1920
Photographer: Unknown
Source: Society for the Preservation of
New England Antiquities

The brick subway kiosk at the left was a landmark in the square from the opening of the subway in 1912 until a new kiosk was installed in 1928. The kiosk shown here was not without its critics. About the time of this view, the Harvard Square Businessmen's Association had petitioned for its removal; they claimed that its bulk and lack of a perimeter sidewalk was a grave traffic hazard. The combination of trolleys, automobiles, and pedestrians at a busy intersection impeded by the large kiosk caused traffic problems not unlike those of the present. The most prominent feature of the new kiosk was the large copper roof with a generous overhang. The structure was made effectively transparent by the architect's use of thin brick piers and glass infill.

The ever-increasing activity in Harvard Square stimulated new construction in the early twentieth century. The four-story Abot Building, in the center of the photograph at the junction of Kennedy (formerly Boylston) and Brattle streets, was built in 1908.

The Charles River Trust Company had been housed in the southern section of College House, but in 1916 a portion of that building was demolished in order to build the Georgian Revival structure at the right. To the left of the bank building, Lyceum Hall, housing the Harvard Cooperative Society, was in its last years; it would soon be replaced by a new structure erected by the Harvard Cooperative Society.

54 *Harvard Square from the Coop*

Location: 1400 Massachusetts Avenue, looking east
Date: c. 1925
Photographer: Unknown
Source: Cambridge Chamber of Commerce

ह~

This view from the vestibule of the Harvard Cooperative Society shows the increasing uniformity of Harvard Square during the 1920s with the construction of several Georgian Revival commercial and academic buildings, most notably Lehman Hall, in the center behind the subway kiosk, and the Harvard Cooperative Society building, both erected in 1924.

The Harvard Cooperative Society was organized in 1882 by Harvard undergraduates as an alternative to the high prices of Harvard Square stores. The business originally occupied several shelves in a fruit shop in College House. A month later, the society moved around the square to Drury's tobacco shop in Holyoke House, where the student traffic was better. During these early years the society sold new books and supplies at a two-thirds discount; in addition, it sold second-hand goods and stored old books and furniture for members.

In October 1883 the society moved to larger quarters in Dane Hall, the former law school building. When in the early twentieth century the college became concerned about losing its tax-exempt status, the administration asked the Harvard Cooperative Society to move out of Harvard-owned property. The society purchased Lyceum Hall in 1903 for $77,500, taking possession completely in 1904, and in 1924 the present Coop building was erected on the site.

Massachusetts Institute of Technology
Location: Massachusetts Avenue
near Memorial Drive
Date: 1915
Photographer: Unknown
Source: M.I.T. Museum

The main complex of the Massachusetts Institute of Technology is shown with construction almost completed.

The institute, founded in 1860, was originally located at Copley Square in Boston. As the student population grew in the late nineteenth century, more space was needed than was available there. In 1912, the institute bought forty-three acres of land in Cambridge on the north bank of the Charles River, east of Massachusetts Avenue, an area where the Charles River seawall had been built and land recently filled in. The land had remained undeveloped after the collapse of the Charles River Embankment Company in the depression of 1893; Charles Davenport's scheme to transform this section of the riverfront into a luxury residential area with parks and promenades had never come to pass.

Welles Bosworth, an 1889 alumnus of M.I.T. and a successful New York architect, was commissioned to design the new campus. In 1912 Bosworth designed the main complex shown here, drawing on the Beaux Arts classical tradition, with a central pavilion housing the library and extended wings around major courtyards. Both this complex and the Walker Memorial to the east, also designed by Bosworth, were oriented toward the Charles River and Boston.

These early M.I.T. buildings, constructed between 1913 and 1917, formed the eastern part of the campus. Much of the institute's later development was to the west and across Massachusetts Avenue.

56 *F. H. Davis Display Car*

Location: Intersection of Garden and
Mason streets
Date: 1918
Photographer: Unknown
Source: F. H. Davis Company

ॐ

The F. H. Davis display car was part
of a World War I Liberty Loan Parade.
The car was driven by John J. Hansen,
the company foreman for many years.
Like many other Cambridge businesses, the F. H. Davis Company was
proud of its wartime participation;
thirty percent of its employees had
been in service and the company had
supported the war effort through the
purchase of war bonds.

The F. H. Davis Company was
located in the northwest part of the
city near the Fitchburg Railroad line, at
175 Richdale Avenue. Founded in
1889, the company specialized in paper-mill machinery, steam engines,
pumps, and machine tools. The F. H.
Davis Company is still on Richdale
Avenue, in a brick structure dating
from around 1905, and sells recon-
ditioned paper-mill machinery.

57 *World War I Victory Parade*

Location: Massachusetts Avenue west
of Prospect Street
Date: 1919–1920
Photographer: Unknown
Source: Raymond L. Patten

More than 8,000 Cambridge men
served in the military during World
War I. Their return from Europe was
the occasion for celebrations and
parades. The expansive mood of these
celebrations was buoyed by an economic victory on the home front,
where industrial growth had been
rapid during the war. The value of
Cambridge's industrial products was
$50 million in 1910; by the end of the
war that figure had doubled.

The fervor shown in this victory
parade had been matched by the inten-
sity of the Cambridge war effort. During the war years Harvard had been a
major center of military activity, with
R.O.T.C. classes taught by French
officers. The freshman dormitories
were used for barracks, while other
barracks covered the Common. A
number of college buildings had been
taken over for the establishment of a
Naval Radio School. More than 11,000
Harvard students and alumni enlisted,
swelling the ranks of Cambridge men
active in World War I.

58 *Engine 2, Lafayette Square Fire Station*

Location: Lafayette Square, 378 Massachusetts Avenue
Date: c. 1920
Photographer: Dennis R. Sullivan
Source: Mrs. Helen Lawrence

ૐ

Supplanting the early volunteer societies, the Cambridge Fire Department had been organized in 1832 with six hand engines and one hand ladder truck. By 1847, the city had a reservoir system and firehouses with professional firemen. As the city grew and prospered, more firehouses were added, including the Lafayette Square firehouse, which was built in 1893. The building was designed by Condon & Greco for horse-drawn equipment, but was later adapted to the motorized equipment that was introduced around 1914. The Lafayette Square firehouse is still in use.

Dennis Sullivan, the photographer, was a fireman who worked first as a laborer for the city before joining the Cambridge Fire Department in 1901. He was a driver at a number of different stations before becoming a lieutenant in the fire department in 1920. He was made a captain by 1926. An amateur photographer, Sullivan recorded many of the city's firemen, their fire stations, and fire equipment in the early 1900s.

59 *Swartz Brothers, Furriers*
Location: 1199 Cambridge Street
Date: 1928–1929
Photographer: Unknown
Source: Maxwell Swartz

ॐ
_____

Myers Swartz, on the far right, emigrated to the United States with his brother Louis in order to escape conscription in the Russian Army. They both came to Cambridge and were later joined by a third brother, Jack.

Louis started a grocery business on Elm Street, while Myers was apprenticed to a furrier in Boston. By 1923, Myers had started his own business along with his brother Jack, who is seated behind the typewriter in this photograph. The two brothers first worked in the front room of Myers's apartment on Cambridge Street at the corner of Windsor Street. By 1925 they had enough orders to be able to rent this shop at 1199 Cambridge Street. Later, they moved to 1820 Massachusetts Avenue, at the corner of Mt. Vernon Street, where Swartz Brothers, Furriers, was located until the 1950s.

Myers made frequent trips to Brazil to purchase ocelot and nutria furs. He learned to speak Portuguese, which was useful because the Swartz brothers employed Portuguese women, many of whom did not speak English, to sew linings into fur coats. Some of the most popular coats in the 1920s were seal and mink, with raccoon coats the favorite among the local college students.

60 *Lechmere Canal*

Location: East Cambridge, looking
north from Commercial Avenue
Date: 1920
Photographer: Unknown
Source: Metropolitan District Commission

Constructed after 1900, the Lechmere Canal is one of two survivors of a series of canals built to take advantage of Cambridge's river location. Shown here is the canal and the East Cambridge industries that settled alongside it.

The first canal system in the city was begun in Cambridgeport in the early 1800s, after congress declared Cambridge a Port of Entry; however, the Embargo of 1807 and the War of 1812 destroyed the commercial prospects of the Broad Canal and little development took place until after the Civil War. The eventual success of the Broad Canal and the increasing industrialization of East Cambridge provided an incentive to fill more of the Charles River tidal flats. In 1900, the Harbor Commissioners granted John T. Scully permission to construct bulkheads and walls to form the Lechmere Canal. Scully used part of the former

shoreline, which remained after the land around First Street and Commercial Avenue had been reclaimed from the mud flats in the 1890s.

Scully's new canal ran parallel to the Craigie Bridge as far west as First Street and then turned south toward Bent Street. The south side of the approach to Craigie's Bridge had been partially filled in during the 1830s and was already lined with wharves for lumber, coal, and stone-cutting businesses that used the waterfront for transport of goods. The new Lechmere Canal allowed these businesses to continue undisturbed.

At the west end of the canal was the E. D. Sawyer Lumber Company. Schooners like the one in the center had been bringing lumber from Maine since the early nineteenth century. In

1920 E. D. Sawyer was the largest lumberyard in the area, but there were two other lumber companies, as well as three coal yards and a marble company, along Lechmere Canal at this period.

The south side of the canal, in the foreground, remained undeveloped for many years. Although lots on this side of the Lechmere Canal had both water and land access along Commercial Avenue, the land was still held by Scully's heirs in 1920 and was not developed until after World War II.

In the background are several significant late-nineteenth- and early-twentieth-century East Cambridge industries. The three-story brick building at the far left was the Cambridge Street building of the Irving and Casson–A. H. Davenport Company, a nationally known supplier of interior furnishings for homes and public buildings from 1883 to the 1950s. The structure with the square tower was the main building of the Revere Sugar Refinery, which began operations in 1871 on Water Street, near Miller's

River. The tallest chimney in the photograph was the 1851 stack of the New England Glass Company, the first major industry in East Cambridge. Although the factory had closed in 1889, the West End Street Railway owned the property and kept the buildings standing until 1921. At the far right of the photograph is the roundhouse of the Boston & Lowell Railroad, built around the turn of the century as part of the railroad's main yards, which extended from East Cambridge to Charlestown. All of these buildings have been demolished.

61 *Ralph A. Trodella at John Reardon & Sons*

Location: 54 Waverly Street
Date: c. 1920
Photographer: Unknown
Source: Alice Owens

Ralph A. Trodella, who came to this country around 1905 from Italy, is in the foreground, working at the John Reardon & Sons rendering business at 54 Waverly Street. The company was founded by an earlier immigrant to Cambridge. John Reardon came from Ireland with his wife, and by 1856 had established his tallow business on Erie Street in Cambridge. His two sons, Edmund and James, joined the business in 1863. The company exported tallow to England and the Continent, as well as to New England, New York, Pennsylvania, and the Southern states.

In 1878 the Reardon company moved to an acre of filled land near Fort Washington, where a new factory was built on the Boston & Albany Railroad to accommodate a business that had expanded beyond tallow to include soap and oleomargarine. By 1896 John Reardon & Sons had added glycerine, ground bone, and fertilizer to their product line. The neighborhood around the factory where many soap workers lived was known derisively as "Greasy Village."

John Reardon died in 1883, and James in 1887; Edmund carried on the family business after their deaths. John Reardon & Sons continued in operation into the early 1960s.

Holy Ghost Society

Location: Unknown
Date: 1927–1928
Photographer: Park Studio
Source: Catherine Kenney

&~

The Holy Ghost Society of St. Anthony's Church is a religious organization of lay Catholics that continues today.

Frank Oliver, shown second from the left in the back row, was a member of the Holy Ghost Society in the 1920s. Born Francisco Oliveira about 1865 in the Azores, he was one of many Portuguese immigrants who came to Cambridge during the early part of the twentieth century. After arriving in the United States and anglicizing his name, Frank Oliver first lived in Rhode Island and then moved to East Cambridge about 1918. He settled near other Portuguese families in that area and worked for the American Net and Twine Company on Second Street, making fish nets.

63 *Noon Athletic Event*

Location: George F. Blake Company,
265 Third Street
Date: c. 1925
Photographer: Unknown
Source: Cambridge YMCA

è≥

In addition to its regular athletic program, the Cambridge YMCA sponsored noon athletic events at some of
the city's largest companies. Such an
event is shown here at the George F.
Blake Company in East Cambridge.
The Blake company employed many
of the city's newly arrived immigrants;
a large number of Blake workers were
from Lithuania, Poland, and Portugal.

George F. Blake had patented the
first steam pump in 1862 while employed as a mechanical engineer at
Peter Hubbell's brickyard in Cambridge. He founded the George F.
Blake Company in 1874. The firm was
well known for its manufacture of a
variety of pumps, including a steam
pump designed for pumping water out
of clay pits. By 1889, the company occupied nearly six acres of land between
Second, Bent, Third, and Binney
streets.

May Day

Location: Memorial Drive,
Mt. Auburn and Hawthorne streets
Date: c. 1925
Photographer: Herbert W. Taylor
Source: Cambridge Recreation Department

ટે≤

These schoolchildren dancing around
the Maypole typify the American ver-
sion of May Day festivities. Many
such festivals were organized for
schoolchildren by the Cambridge Recreation Department during the Twen-
ties. In addition to the May Day
celebration, the department sponsored
mock jousts with a medieval theme,
patriotic pageants, and regular play-
groups at parks and playgrounds
throughout the city.

Herbert Whyte Taylor, the photographer, ran a studio at 349 Harvard
Street in Cambridge from 1909 to
1927. Taylor's work received attention in *Photo Era Magazine* in 1899,
which called him "one of the most
sensitively artistic of modern
photographers."

V 1930–1945

65 *Harvard Houses*

Location: Charles River from Dunster
House to Weeks Bridge
Date: 1936
Photographer: Unknown
Source: Harvard University Archives

Lowell House, McKinlock Hall, Dunster House, and the other Georgian Revival structures shown were all designed by Coolidge, Shepley, Bulfinch & Abbott during the massive Harvard building program of the early twentieth century.

During the administration of President A. Lawrence Lowell, from 1904 to 1933, Harvard's physical plant changed dramatically. The university undertook a vast building program on the riverfront, which represented a major change in university housing policy. Under President Eliot, students had been expected to arrange their own housing, but President Lowell instituted the house system, based on a more traditional form of scholastic community, in which students and professors live in close contact in residential colleges. The house system has been the basis of Harvard undergraduate life since the late 1920s.

The administration chose the Georgian Revival style for the riverfront houses in an effort to extend Harvard Yard's atmosphere to these new dormitory buildings.

66 *South Side of Harvard Square*

Location: 1372 Massachusetts Avenue
Date: c. 1935
Photographer: Unknown
Source: Cambridge Savings Bank

ॐ≽

By the 1930s, Harvard Square had developed an intensely metropolitan character. The completion of the subway in 1912 brought on a wave of construction that all but eliminated the remaining wooden buildings. The new structures were of brick, generally in the Georgian Revival style and several stories high. Cambridge was now connected by subway and telephone with downtown Boston and the other great urban areas of the Northeast, and had lost the small-town atmosphere it had retained through World War I. There was no major physical change in the appearance of the square until Holyoke House, seen here on the left, was replaced by Holyoke Center in 1961; little else changed until the subway extension began in 1978.

The Cambridge Savings Bank, incorporated in 1834, was the twentieth savings bank in the state. After operating at several locations in Harvard Square during most of the nineteenth century, it built a new building on Dunster Street in 1897. In part a private dormitory known as Dana Chambers, the new offices proved unsatisfactory and in 1924 the bank built its present building in a prominent location facing Harvard Square.

Adjacent to the bank is a three-story commercial building that hides three of Harvard Square's oldest structures, of which the most prominent was Farwell's General Store (c. 1790). In 1896 the buildings were joined and their facades remodeled to their present appearance.

67 *Cambridge Gas & Electric Company*

Location: 23 Church Street
Date: 1936
Photographer: Unknown
Source: Cambridge Gas & Electric Company

&

This publicity photograph of the Cambridge Gas & Electric Company's new office in Harvard Square shows the firm's dramatic nighttime display of the latest in kitchen appliances for the New Deal era. These offices were actually late-nineteenth-century carriage shops that were reduced to one story and covered by a new facade in 1936. Cambridge architect William B. Galvin, the foremost practitioner of the Art Moderne Style in the city, used streamlined neon tubing on the facade to highlight the cast-concrete entry. In its low, horizontal form—a marked contrast to the company's formal Renaissance Revival headquarters in Central Square—the neon-lit Harvard Square office resembled contemporary structures of Miami or Los Angeles more than those of Cambridge or Boston.

Galvin was trained as an architect at Harvard, graduating in 1931. He began his career with Neo-Georgian designs, such as the Oxford Ale House, located diagonally across from this building, at 36 Church Street. However, with his 1931 Art Deco design for Shea Cleaners at 1016 Massachusetts Avenue (now demolished), Galvin achieved a reputation for an innovative popular style, which lasted through the Depression. His later buildings prior to World War II included his offices at 38 Brattle Street, as well as two outstanding mid Cambridge apartment blocks at 10 Forest Street and 36 Highland Avenue.

Although stripped of its original neon, this structure at 23 Church Street remains intact. It is the finest example of the Moderne Style in Harvard Square and a legacy of Galvin's streamlined imagination.

68 *Traffic Booth*

Location: Harvard Square
Date: c. 1945
Photographer: Unknown
Source: Cambridge Engineering
Department

ટે

Stationed with microphone in hand,
the policemen in the traffic booths at
Central and Harvard squares were a
Cambridge institution in the postwar
years. As traffic patterns became more
complex at these busy intersections, directions barked at passing motorists
and pedestrians helped diminish the
chaos. This photograph is of a temporary booth on the north side of Harvard Square; the permanent booth that
replaced it lasted until about 1967. The
officer shown is Charles Martin, who
joined the force in 1926 and retired
in 1957.

69 *Nonstop Drive*

Location: Cambridge Motor Company,
277 Massachusetts Avenue
Date: 1933
Photographer: Roy J. Jacoby
Source: Walter R. Hahn

The nonstop drive was a promotional
venture of the thirties, like a dance
marathon, sponsored by Cambridge
businesses. Local advertisements deco-
rate the car, which posed at the beginning of its run in front of the Cambridge Motor Company. How long
the car toured Cambridge with its
loudspeaker blaring is not known, but
it is certain that the novelty wore off
quickly.

Most prominent of the advertisers is
that of Hahn's Bakery. Jacob Hahn
came to Cambridge in 1926 after opening bakeries in Boston and Dorchester,
and started Hahn's Bakery at 243
Hampshire Street. His business prospered, and in 1931 he added another
bakery, at 15 Pearl Street in Central
Square. His son Walter eventually took
over the business.

Roy J. Jacoby was a Boston commercial photographer.

70 *Bank Teller and Customer*
Location: Cambridgeport Savings
Bank, 689 Massachusetts Avenue
Date: c. 1930
Photographer: Fairfield Studio(?)
Source: Cambridgeport Savings Bank

ౖ❧

The Cambridgeport Savings Bank, incorporated in 1853, has always been
located near Central Square on Massachusetts Avenue. In 1904 the bank
hired architects W. E. Chamberlin and
C. H. Blackall to design their neoclas-
sical structure at 689 Massachusetts
Avenue, the interior of which is shown
here.

The Cambridgeport Savings Bank is
the third known structure on this site.
It was preceeded by a building used as
the *Cambridge Chronicle* office in 1855
and a Masonic Hall built in 1865 by
the architect N. J. Bradlee. Still occupying the 1904 structure, the Cambridgeport Savings Bank has shared
the building with the Harvard Trust
Company since shortly after construction was completed.

This photograph was one of a series
of publicity photographs probably
taken by a photographer from the
Fairfield Studio in Boston.

71 *Malone's Pharmacy*

Location: 1770 Massachusetts Avenue
Date: c. 1935
Photographer: Harold Willoughby &
Associates
Source: Cambridge Electric Light Company

ے

The Cambridge Electric Light Company's photograph collection contains a series of images that were taken to demonstrate the effectiveness of electric spotlights for retail storefront displays.

Edward A. Malone started his drugstore at the corner of Lancaster Street in 1921 or 1922. The drugstore was in a block of one-story, brick retail stores on Massachusetts Avenue between Lancaster and Linnaean streets that still stands. The stores were built about 1920 and were remodeled as one continuous block in 1930. Malone's pharmacy continued until the 1960s at the same location, with John J. Malone eventually taking over his father's business.

Harold Willoughby & Associates was a studio active in Boston from 1928 until 1947.

72 **Portuguese Liberty Band**
Location: Clerk of Courts Building,
Otis and Second streets
Date: 1934
Photographer: Unknown
Source: Mary Ferreira

ટ✍

The Portuguese Liberty Band, formed in the late 1920s, existed until the late 1960s. The band was sponsored by the Portuguese Liberty Club, one of the oldest organizations in the Cambridge Portuguese community. This fraternal organization had its first headquarters on Cambridge Street in East Cambridge and then moved to the Inman Square building at 1348 Cambridge Street. Many of its members were recent immigrants, who eventually became American citizens. The band played for religious feasts, parades, and patriotic occasions.

This photograph was taken on the occasion of St. Anthony's Feast in 1934, when the band members had just received new uniforms. Nicholas Marvro, in civilian clothes at the right, was the conductor.

73 *Paradise Spa*

Location: 352 Cambridge Street
Date: 1931
Photographer: Unknown
Source: Manuel Rogers, Sr.

ࢶ

Manuel Rogers, Sr., shown behind the counter, owned the Paradise Spa between 1927 and 1942. Located in the heart of the Portuguese community in East Cambridge, the spa was a favorite place for young people, who often gathered after school in the back room where there were booths and a jukebox.

Manuel Rogers, Sr., whose parents emigrated from the Azores, grew up in Cambridge at the corner of Charles and Fourth streets. Rogers later opened a funeral home on Cambridge Street. He died in 1984.

Wartime Rationing
Location: Unknown
Date: c. 1944
Photographer: James P. Dromey
Source: Eugenia M. Dromey

ﺑﺴ

During World War II, shortages of
consumer items caused the government
to institute a rationing system based on
coupon books that contained "points."
Consumers all over the country were
given a small number of "points" to
buy the scarcest grocery items, particularly red meat. Other items, such as
canned vegetables, were more readily
available, while fresh produce was not
rationed at all. Here Eugenia Dromey
surveys the goods available at a Cambridge market.

75 *Fireworks Stand*

Location: 350-352 Cambridge Street
Date: 1939
Photographer: Unknown
Source: Manuel Rogers, Sr.

છે

Manuel Rogers, Sr., is just visible behind the temporary fireworks stand that he operated on Cambridge Street in 1938 and 1939. During those years, Rogers set up a collapsible stand on a driveway beside the Paradise Spa at 350 Cambridge Street to sell fireworks for patriotic holidays such as the Fourth of July and Bunker Hill Day.

Rogers purchased the fireworks from a company in Brighton. His stock included Roman candles, ladyfingers, two-inch salutes, and sparklers. Fireworks displays were a favorite part of summer holiday amusement and the business was profitable enough for Rogers to buy a washing machine for his wife with the first summer's proceeds.

Fireworks stands became a thing of the past with the outlawing of fireworks in 1943.

76 *Dr. Edwin Land*

Location: Osborne Street
Date: 1946
Photographer: Unknown
Source: Polaroid Corporation

છે

Dr. Edwin Land, the inventor of instant photography and founder of the Polaroid Corporation, has been responsible for some of the most original advances in camera design and film technology in the twentieth century. In 1932, while a student at Harvard, Land developed a means of producing synthetic light polarizing material. He left Harvard that year to explore the commercial applications of his invention, and in 1937 formed the Polaroid Corporation. Among the firm's early products were photographic filters, optical devices, and a three-dimensional motion picture system. Beginning with a flash of insight in 1944, he quickly developed the technology of one-step photography. A complete camera system was made available to the public in 1948.

This photograph, one of the first using the new process, was made in 1946 on Osborne Street outside Dr. Land's laboratory at 708 Main Street. This was not the earliest scientific activity on the site; in 1873, Alexander Graham Bell and Thomas Watson, his assistant, made the first reciprocal telephone call between a previous building and Bell's laboratory in Boston. Portions of this industrial complex date to the 1840s, when the railroad car works of Charles Davenport were located here.

VI George K. Warren,
Cambridge Photographer

George Kendall Warren's long career began in 1851 in Lowell, Massachusetts, and spanned the transition from the early daguerreotypes printed on silver-coated metal plates to the development of modern photographic methods. His daguerrean studio in Cambridge, opened in 1863, was one of the city's first. Active professionally in Cambridge for nearly twenty years, Warren was renowned for the quality of his portrait work; celebrities of all sorts sought out his studios to be immortalized by his camera. During most of his Cambridge career, Warren also specialized in college-album photography. He was commissioned by many colleges over the course of two decades, but he is remembered primarily for the work he produced during the years he served as the class-album photographer for Harvard College. His photographs are an invaluable record of Harvard College and the Cambridge community in the late nineteenth century.

George Kendall Warren was born in 1834 in Nashua, New Hampshire, the son of John Banks Warren, a textile worker, and his wife, Rebecca. Within a few years of George's birth, the Warren family moved to Lowell, Massachusetts. Lowell was a young, flourishing city with a rapidly growing textile industry that offered generous benefits and competitive salaries to attract workers to the new mills.[1] The Warrens probably made the fifteen-mile move from Nashua so that John Warren could work in the Boott Corporation cotton mill, which had opened in Lowell in 1835, for by 1855 John Banks Warren was an overseer, or foreman, at Boott and he and his family were living in one of the company's houses.

George Warren grew up in Lowell and attended school there. Although the Warrens were not a particularly wealthy family, Warren managed to attend high school. This was unusual in the 1850s, especially in Lowell, where most children began working in the mills shortly after the seventh or eighth grade.[2] Warren probably did not graduate, since the Lowell high school awarded its first diplomas in 1858; however, his relatively long schooling indicates the economic prosperity John Banks Warren had achieved with the Boott Corporation.

When he finished school, Warren decided to become a daguerreotypist; in 1851 his parents invested in a daguerrean studio for him at 128 Merrimac Street, in the business center of Lowell. Warren's first months in this still new career—the daguerreotype had been invented in France in 1839, and became popular in America during the 1840s—were a time of experimentation and discouragement. Florence Howe, in her 1959 *Yankee Magazine* article, "George Kendall Warren: His Agile Camera," draws on the diary of Warren's mother, Rebecca, for details of these early months when George tested various chemicals and crude equipment, trying to produce creditable daguerreotypes of family and friends. Despite new equipment bought to facilitate his work, Warren faced failure after failure in his attempts to silver his own daguerrean plates. Rebecca Warren's journal indicates the strong support she offered her son as he tried to establish himself in this new field:

Pierian Sodality

Location: Unknown
Date: 1869
Photographer: George K. Warren
Source: Harvard University Archives

Natural History Society
Location: Harvard Yard
Date: 1865
Photographer: George K. Warren
Source: Robert Severy

area.[8] Warren was especially innovative and successful in capturing the odd, nonacademic personalities around Harvard Square. His 1861 and 1862 albums contain pictures of "Professor" Abram Molineaux, the gymnasium instructor; Picolo, the cigar boy; Clary, the black janitor at Boylston Hall; Lexie, the class dog; and the College Goodies, the haggard, wizened women who cleaned the students' rooms. Most of Warren's portrait work was printed in an oval format; the scenes of Cambridge or views of buildings were often in a rectangular format. Over the years Warren added to the photographs of personalities and local scenes available to the students: in 1861, his first year, he offered 155 photographs; by 1866 there were 252 photographs, including more character portraits, such as J. L. Haddow, the barber, and Tommy, the paperhanger.

Harvard class albums were handsome, folio-sized volumes composed only of photographs. They were bound in leather and decorated in gold, with gilt-edged pages. Many of these early albums, which are in the Harvard University Archives, weigh as much as twenty or thirty pounds, because of the thick stock on which the pictures are mounted. An average album of the period contained about 125 4½-by-6½-inch, cabinet-sized portraits of students, along with about fifteen portraits of professors, approximately the same number of views of campus buildings or locales, and four or five portraits of favorite campus characters. However, the albums ranged from some consisting solely of pictures of graduates and faculty to those including views of nearly every building on the Harvard campus.

At Harvard, the production of these albums was the responsibility of the graduating class, which selected a committee to contract with a photographer of its choice. Each year, Warren, or whoever was the chosen photographer, took pictures of the graduates. Initially, at least, he also took pictures of the faculty, and various campus spots and personalities. If he were retained in future years, as Warren often was, these photographs were used again and again. Warren would update his Harvard collection every few years, adding new views of present campus favorites and discarding outdated ones. The images belonged to Harvard, however. If in subsequent years a new photographer was chosen, he often used these earlier pictures, sometimes reshooting them in another format but sometimes merely stamping his name on the back. Warren's pictures of the College Goodies, for example, reappear throughout the 1860s and 1870s, although Harvard changed photographers four times in those years.

The albums were custom-made for each student. In the middle of the spring, a leaflet listing the photographs available that year would be circulated among the students. For a price per photograph, the student would check off the ones he wanted on the list and return his selections to either the class committee or the photographer. The chosen photographs would be bound and the student's name embossed in gold on the cover. Each student thus had a personalized record of his Harvard years.

Although Warren's college-album business appeared to thrive throughout the 1860s, in the 1870s his focus shifted. At the beginning of the decade he began working exclusively with the new albumen prints, abandoning daguerreotypes, which had dominated his earlier work. In 1870, while maintaining his Cambridge studio and his college-album work, he opened a studio at 145 Tremont Street, the business center of Boston, where the most elegant and prominent photographic galleries were located. Apparently having decided he was ready to take on another, perhaps more lucrative market, Warren began to distinguish himself as a portrait photographer; the number of celebrities among his clients increased. As an outgrowth of his portrait work, Warren also became involved in the production of curiosity cards, mass-produced pictures of celebrities of all types, which were collected to be put into albums or traded much in the manner that baseball cards are now collected and traded by children.

These cards were a byproduct of the switch from the more expensive silver-coated daguerrean plates to the relatively inexpensive paper prints of modern photography. Portraits, even of obscure individuals, could now be printed on small cards (the size varied from one photographer to another), which could be left as calling cards or *cartes de visite*. Portraits of celebrities in such form quickly became collectors' items, generating a new line of business.

At about the same time Warren took up portrait work, his college-album business began to taper off. Although he retained some college accounts until 1877, the middle of the 1870s saw a rapid decline in his ability to secure college clients. The reasons for Warren's withdrawal from the work that had provided such a steady part of his business are not known, although the vagaries of such a clientele are readily apparent, since the photographer remained dependent upon the senior-class committees whose members were different each year. William Welling, in an analysis of the college class photographers of the late nineteenth century in his *Photography in America*, quotes the New York *World* as having maintained that "The photographer who bases his calculations on the likelihood of retaining the patronage of a given college for a long series of years is tolerably certain, whatever the degree of his artistic success, to come to grief at the end."[9] It is a testament to Warren's artistic achievement that he was retained by Harvard and other colleges for so many years.

But by 1874 there were notices of dissatisfaction with Warren's college work. In that year, the Harvard *Magenta*, forerunner of the *Crimson*, noted Yale's disappointment with Warren's work. Then, in 1877, when Warren was again contracted by Harvard after a lapse of five years, the editors of the *Crimson*, displeased with his straightforward, conventional portraits, printed this stinging editorial:

The prevalent feeling in the class of seventy-seven in regard to Mr. Warren's photographic efforts is decidedly one of disappointment. Perhaps it is safe to say that much was not expected; for the selection of the committee was at the very best but a leap in the dark, and nobody had any expectation of landing on *terra firma*. Certain it is that if by *terra firma* is meant good and faithful work, the result shows a wide gap between land and water. For ourselves we saw at the time no reason why Mr. Notman should be cast aside and the self-styled Cambridgeport "Celebrity Photographer" should be employed in a work which requires tact, taste, and skill. By remembering just where a

79 *Molineaux, the Gym Instructor*
Location: Unknown
Date: 1864
Photographer: George K. Warren
Source: Harvard University Archives

80 *Picolo, the Cigar Boy*
Location: Unknown
Date: 1864
Photographer: George K. Warren
Source: Harvard University Archives

man sat in a group picture we have been able after much study to recognize a few lineaments of one or two of our most intimate friends. One man, with whose clear, bright eye we were all familiar, comes out under the "Celebrity Photographer's" manipulation Homeric in his blindness. Another, whose mild, good-natured countenance is almost proverbial, by some mysterious process is changed into a hardened *roué* just returned after ten years' dissipation on the Continent. Another's is very good, if considered as an ambitious *study*, but is very little of a likeness. In early Greek art it was customary to have the name of the subject printed under the picture. In this infancy of photographic art we recommend to have each man's name stamped in heavy capitals under his picture. Again, in attending to orders by mail, Memorial waiters, chemistry tutors, or college scouts have been stupidly returned for such men as Mr. Lowell, Norton, Bowen, or Goodwin. We have no personal feeling against the "Celebrity Photographer," but we feel it our duty to warn any succeeding class against such negligence, lack of taste, and incapacity as the Cambridgeport "Celebrity Photographer" has shown.[10]

1877 marked the end of Warren's long association with Harvard, and indeed, with college-album work.

However, as Warren's college work declined through the 1870s, his portrait business expanded. Warren changed the location of his Boston studio several times, moving in 1872 from Tremont Street to 289 Washington Street, and in 1875 to a studio at 465 Washington Street, which he operated until 1882. Like Warren, many nineteenth-century photographers were entrepreneurs as much as technicians or artists, opening many studios and employing dozens of people. In changing studios as Warren did, photographers often bought already existing ones, purchasing equipment, negatives, and chemicals rather than going to the expense of renovating and stocking a studio.

As Warren's celebrity portrait business increased he hired several assistants to help manage the business. The best of these was probably Sumner B. Heald, who first worked with Warren at the Tremont Street studio and was made superintendent of the new Washington Street studio in 1872. Under Heald's supervision, the 289 Washington Street studio turned out many superb portraits of celebrities, the work for which Warren received the greatest recognition in his own day. It is difficult to know whether Warren himself or his studio superintendents had primary responsibility for the photographs the studios turned out; while the studio managers were also photographers and may have operated the camera, all work produced was printed with the studio name. Heald remained Warren's superintendent until 1875, when Warren closed the first Washington Street studio; Heald went on to form a partnership with another photographer. Among the portraits produced under Heald's supervision at 289 Washington Street were those of Colonel Thomas Wentworth Higginson, writer and social reformer; M. M. Ballou, the publisher of the *Boston Globe*; Charlotte Cushman, "the most powerful actress America has ever produced"; and John Albion Andrews, the governor of Massachusetts during the Civil War.[11]

Warren took more portraits, especially of celebrities, in the new studio at 465 Washington Street, opened in 1875, than in any of his other studios. Among those photographed here were Edward Everett Hale, William Dean Howells, John Greenleaf Whittier, P. T. Barnum, Helen Hunt Jackson, Louisa May Alcott, Mary Mapes Dodge, William Lloyd Garrison, J. G. Holland, George M. Pullman, Mark Twain, J. T. Fields, Henry Wadsworth Longfellow, Charles W. Eliot, Lucy Stone, James Russell Lowell, and Harriet Beecher Stowe.[12]

Despite his success, Warren did not abandon attempts to improve his technical and artistic expertise. In 1877 the *Boston Post* cited Warren for his experiments in photographing by electric light. Warren was one of many New Englanders in that period to experiment with the effects of electric light, including John Whipple, who in 1863 had illuminated the Boston Common with an electric arc in order to take photographs.[13]

Warren's continuing progress in photography is evidenced by a bronze medal from the 1878 Mechanics' Exhibition in Boston for his "large collection of cabinets of celebrated authors, actors, etc."[14] Although the judges did not find "evidence of a decided advance in portrait photography from the exhibition of four years [earlier] . . . the best work [showed] more skill and taste in posing the figures, arranging accessories, and improvements in printing, mounting, and general finish."

Warren seems not to have limited his enterprise to photography. The *Boston Traveller*, in a review of the 1878 exhibition published on October 30, 1878, called attention to the "superb contributions from Mr. Warren's studio drawn by his artist, Mr. Engels." The *Traveller* continued: "Mr. Warren's exhibit has been divided into three sections—photographs, water colors and crayons—and he is the only photographer who has been admitted into the art gallery. Warren's portrait of Miss Lillian Conway is singled out for praise, as is another portrait. The review concludes:

. . . In fact, it has been said that Mr. Warren gives more character to his pictures than any now in New England, and as is well known scarcely a prominent person passes through the city without giving him a sitting. His studio at No. 465 Washington is most conveniently located, and it seems useless to add is well worth a visit. Mr. C. B. Ayer is the gentlemanly and courteous manager of the theatrical and celebrity department, and is constantly producing pictures which are sold all over this country and in Europe. All classes of work both in oil painting, crayon drawings, as well as photography in all of its branches . . . done at very reasonable rates, and the public may secure fine work at prices which are extremely moderate.

From these notices of the 1878 Mechanics' Exhibition until his death in a railroad accident late in 1884, little is known about Warren. He continued to maintain his two studios, at 563 Main Street (now 563 Massachusetts Avenue) in Cambridgeport and at 465 Washington Street in Boston, until 1882. In that year, his father died. In the same year, George K. Warren moved his family to Somerville, closed both studios, and opened a new studio at 46 School Street in Boston. This venture could not have been very successful, for by 1883 Warren closed that studio as well. In 1884, he and his family moved to Medford, and he appears to have left the photography business, for he was not listed in the Boston, Cambridge, or Somerville directories of that

81 *The Goodies*

Location: Harvard Hall
Date: 1862
Photographer: George K. Warren
Source: Cambridge Historical Society

year. Warren's actions in the last few years preceding his death were somewhat peculiar; a financial crisis may have been the cause of his behavior. At the time of his death, his personal estate was valued at only $2,400, although this did not include his book accounts or photographic negatives.

George K. Warren died suddenly on November 29, 1884, at age fifty, at the College Hill railroad station in Medford, the victim of an accident involving a Boston & Lowell Railroad train. Boston and Cambridge newspaper reports of his death do not provide the exact circumstances of the accident. After funeral services at Tufts College, Warren was buried at the old cemetery in Medford.

Although he was not a great technical or artistic innovator in the field, George Kendall Warren played an important role in the period when photography developed from something akin to a magic art—"making pictures out of sunshine," as Hawthorne's daguerreotypist hero describes his profession in *The House of the Seven Gables*—into an art form and mode of recording reality, available to many through advances in technology. George K. Warren earned himself a place among nineteenth-century New England photographers, not so much for the portraits of celebrities that brought him the recognition of his contemporaries but for the clear and ample record his work has provided of college and city life in nineteenth-century Cambridge.

Appendix:
Index of Cambridge Commercial
Photographers, 1858–1945

Addresses in parentheses give current
street numbers and names.

Aiken, Frank J.
1873
Cambridge Street, corner Prospect Street

Adams, Kilburn (1858–1905)
1900–1905
1868 Massachusetts Avenue

Admin Photo Studio
1941–1944
649 Massachusetts Avenue, room 6

Alary, Louis
1898
350 Green Street

Andren, Eric L. (1869–1938)
1915–1925
483 Massachusetts Avenue
1926–1928
559 Massachusetts Avenue

Apeda Photo Company
1915
476 Massachusetts Avenue

Arakelyan, Sahag
1918–1920
33 Boylston Street
1921–1930
12 Eliot Street
(See also Harvard Square Studio, Inc.)

Bachrach, Inc.
1944
1416 Massachusetts Avenue, rooms 301,
303, 305

Baltzly, B. F.
1882
Cambridge Street, corner Prescott Street
with G. W. Pach & Bros.
1883
563 Main Street (563 Massachusetts
Avenue)

Barrett, Henry (1848–1913)
1884–1891
110 Cambridge Street (284 Cambridge
Street)
1892–1895
284 Cambridge Street

Belluche Photo Service
1941–1944
180 Franklin Street

Boecker, August C.
1937
18 Brattle Street
1941–1944
18 Brattle Street, room 353, and 46 Con-
cord Avenue

Breda, Joseph
1919
537 Cambridge Street
1920–1922
259 Cambridge Street
1923
46 Second Street
1926–1931
799 Cambridge Street

Brenner, Leon
1917–1918
7 Inman Square

Briand Studio
1944
14 Notre Dame Avenue

Briand, Paul L.
(see Briand Studio)

Buckley, Bertha M.
1915
21 Prospect Street

Buckowski, Walter R.
1921–1922
779 Cambridge Street
1923
729 Cambridge Street
1926–1928
1056 Cambridge Street

Butterfield, David W. (1844–1933)
1882–1903
573 Main Street (573 Massachusetts
Avenue)

Byrd, Edgar L.
1907–1931
1868 Massachusetts Avenue

Byrd Studio
(see Edgar L. Byrd)

Camerlengo, Aristide
1923–1924
1056 Cambridge Street
1925–1927
729 Cambridge Street
1928–1931
539 Cambridge Street
1937–1944
295 Cambridge Street

Camerlengo Photo Studio
(see Aristide Camerlengo)

Cannon, John
1861
Cambridge Street, opposite Post Office

Carlson, Theodore
1899
882 Main Street

Central Studio

1919

649 Massachusetts Avenue

(see also Jacob E. Nathanson)

Central Square Studio

1920

694 Massachusetts Avenue

Chessman, Fred H.

(see Carlos L. Page & Fred H. Chessman)

Chickering, E. Studios, Inc.

1917–1920

32 Boylston Street

Chickering, Elmer

(see E. Chickering Studios, Inc.)

Clough, Omar W.

1890

297 Cambridge Street

Collyer, Frank L.

1914–1916

23 Church Street

1917–1918

12 Boylston Street

Commercial Photo

1911

20 Central Square

1912

10 Pearl Street

Cox, James T.

1912–1913

631 Massachusetts Avenue

(see also Webster Studio, 1914–1918)

Creedman, Benjamin M.

(see Creedman, B. M. Studio and University Studios)

Creedman, B. M. Studio

1937

1109 Massachusetts Avenue

(see also University Studios, 1941–1945)

Danforth, Charles H.

1866–1870

Main Street, corner Magazine Street, Haymarket Square (5 Central Square)

1871

Main Street, corner Magazine Street (5 Central Square)

1872–1873

27 Haymarket Square (5 Central Square)

1874–1878

27 Central Square (5 Central Square)

Dobson, R. A.

1906

12 Brattle Street and 270 Boylston Street, Boston

1907

545 Massachusetts Avenue and 128 Tremont Street, Boston

1908

631 Massachusetts Avenue and 37 Tremont Street, Boston

1909

631 Massachusetts Avenue and 27 Tremont Street, Boston

Elkin, Abraham

(see Apeda Photo Company)

Ellis, Elias

1917

575 Massachusetts Avenue

Ewing, Herbert C.

1908

1286 Massachusetts Avenue, with Notman Studio

Fay, Charles F.

1885

413 Broadway

Gagne, Edward

1895

Windsor Street near Cambridge Street

1896–1901

482 Windsor Street

Galaid, Arthur M.

1921–1922

504 Massachusetts Avenue

Garth, Frederic C.

1896–1898

25 Central Square (5 Central Square)

Glazier, Clarence D. (1872–1934)

1921–1931

649 Massachusetts Avenue

Glazier Studio

(see Clarence D. Glazier, 1930–1931)

Green, Charles R.

1879

573 Main Street (573 Massachusetts Avenue)

Griffin, Daniel A.

1899

7 Bow Street

Griffith, Francis E.

1911

15 Springfield Street

Gustafson, Charles W.

1912–1913

15 Springfield Street

Gutman, Pyser
1920–1923
1279 Cambridge Street

Halberstadt, Ernest
1941
102A Mt. Auburn Street

Haley, Mrs. Catherine
1907
1229 Cambridge Street

Haley, Michael J.
1908
1229 Cambridge Street

Harley & Metcalf
1860–1861
Main Street (Massachusetts Avenue), corner
Inman Street
(see also Harley, Metcalf & Winter)

Harley, Metcalf & Winter
1863–1864
Main Street (Massachusetts Avenue), corner
Magazine Street; also Harvard Square

Harley, Parker C.
(see Harley & Metcalf; Harley, Metcalf &
Winter)

Harvard Square Studio, Inc.
1919–1920
33 Boylston Street
(see also Sahag Arakelyan)

Hatstat, Andrew J.
1888
307 Main Street (Main Street, between
Windsor and Portland streets)

Haywood, John D. (or Heywood)
1865–1866
112 Cambridge Street (Cambridge Street,
between Sciarappa and Third streets)

Hodge, Edward A.
1915–1917
12 Boylston Street

1920
12 Boylston Street

Holbrook, Chester T.
1944
1252 Massachusetts Avenue

Kenney, Cornelius C.
1900
545 Massachusetts Avenue

King, Mrs. Catherine E.
1890
Western Avenue, corner Hews Street

King, Theodore E.
1866–1867
Harvard Square

Larkin, Albin A.
1907
579 Massachusetts Avenue, room 1

Larkins, Alban
1890
Main Street (Massachusetts Avenue), corner
Brookline Street

La Voie, Joseph A.
1931–1941
671 Massachusetts Avenue
(see also La Voie & MacAllister)

La Voie & MacAllister
1926–1928
634 Massachusetts Avenue, room 207
(see also Joseph A. La Voie and Joseph F.
MacAllister)

Lawrentis, Joseph
(see Main Photo Studio)

Leake, Charles R., Jr.
1899
678 Massachusetts Avenue

Lee's Photo Service
1941
298 Massachusetts Avenue

Legg, Frank W.
1879–1881
27 Central Square (5 Central Square)

Leighton's Studio
1906
19 Brattle Street

Levine, Eric
1903–1904
478 Massachusetts Avenue

1905–1909
476 Massachusetts Avenue

1910–1914
483 Massachusetts Avenue

Lewis, Thomas
1875
3 River Street (River Street, corner Franklin
Street)

1876–1880
33 River Street (91 River Street)

Lincoln, Edwin H.
1886–1887
33 River Street (91 River Street)

Lofgren, Gustaf W.
1918
5 Armory Place

Low, Frederick C.
1866–1867
112 Cambridge Street (Cambridge Street between Sciarappa and Third streets)

1868–1883
110 Cambridge Street (Cambridge Street between Sciarappa and Third streets)

1884–1886
27 Central Square (5 Central Square)

Luzackas, Peter (d. 1955)
1911–1925
875 Cambridge Street
(see also Main Photo Studio)

Luzackas & Szczuka
(see Peter Luzackas, 1913; Joseph Szczuka)

Lynch, Mrs. Evangeline T.
1916–1919
620 Cambridge Street

1920–1922
537 and 620 Cambridge Street

Lynch, Frederick John (1865–1919)
1898–1915
620 Cambridge Street

MacAllister, Joseph F.
1930
634 Massachusetts Avenue, room 207
(see also La Voie & MacAllister)

Main Photo Studio
1908
877 Main Street
(see Peter Luzackas, Joseph Lawrentis)

Marshall Studio
1915–1944
4 Brattle Street

Marshall, Wilbert E. (1874–1944)
(see Marshall Studio)

Martain, George E.
1872
Main Street, corner Court Street (Third Street)

Mason, Philip C.
1888–1892
186 North Avenue (Massachusetts Avenue, between Beech and Allen streets)

McCann, John G.
1893–1894
186 North Avenue (Massachusetts Avenue, between Beech and Allen streets)

McClee, Howard P.
1937–1944
76 Garfield Street

Melkon, Onnig D.
1923–1927
550 Massachusetts Avenue

Metcalf, Franklin
(see Harley & Metcalf; Harley, Metcalf & Winter)

Minassian, Arshak D.
(see Admin Photo Studio)

Mitchell, J. S. & Company
1865–1866
Harvard Square

Moore, Albert H.
1917–1920
Harvard University Library

Morse, Benjamin
1910–1911
476 Massachusetts Avenue

Morse, Edwin T. (d. 1897)
1882–1887
Main Street, corner Brewery Street (Technology Square)

1889
311 Main Street (Technology Square)

1890–1891
290 Main Street, (Main Street, between Portland and Albany streets)

1892
310 Main Street (Main Street, between Portland and Albany streets)

Nathanson, Jacob E.
1918–1919
649 Massachusetts Avenue
(see also Central Studio, 1919)

Ness, William T.
1910
1286 Massachusetts Avenue. Manager, Notman Photo Company

1911–1912
1382 Massachusetts Avenue

New England Snapshot Company
1941
678 Massachusetts Avenue, room 401

Nolan, Michael T.
1921–1923
560 Massachusetts Avenue

Nordstrom, Carl
1914–1916
1868 Massachusetts Avenue

Notman, James
1881–1883
7 Brattle Street and 99 Boylston Street, Boston

1884
99 Boylston Street, Boston

1886
400 Harvard Street (1236-1238 Massachusetts Avenue) and 99 Boylston Street, Boston

(see also Notman Photographic Company and Notman Studio)

Notman Photographic Company

1896–1907
1286 Massachusetts Avenue (Notman Studio, 1906-1907)

1910
1286 Massachusetts Avenue

1915–1925
1286 Massachusetts Avenue

(see also James Notman and Notman Studio)

Notman Studio

1906–1907
1286 Massachusetts Avenue

1926–1931
1286 Massachusetts Avenue

(see also James Notman and Notman Photographic Company)

Ohio Photocrafts Company

1928–1930
671 Massachusetts Avenue

Pach, G. W.

(see G. W. Pach & Bros., Pach Brothers)

Pach, G. W. & Bros.

1880–1882
Cambridge Street, corner Prescott Street

1883–1890
Main Street, next to Beck Hall (Massachusetts Avenue, west of Old Cambridge Baptist Church)

(see also Pach Brothers, B. F. Baltzly)

Pach Brothers

1891–1894
Main Street, next to Beck Hall (Massachusetts Avenue, west of Old Cambridge Baptist Church)

1895
1179 Massachusetts Avenue

1896–1916
1181 Massachusetts Avenue

(see also G. W. Pach & Bros., H. William Tupper)

Page, Carlos L.

1861
Wood's Block, Main Street (573 Massachusetts Avenue)

(see also Carlos L. Page & Fred H. Chessman)

Page, Carlos L. & Chessman, Fred H.

1860
Wood's Block, Main Street (573 Massachusetts Avenue)

(see also Carlos L. Page)

Pariseau, H. A.

1908
26 York Street

Park Studio

1926–1944
875 Cambridge Street

Parker, Edgar O.

1917
15 Brattle Street

1918–1923
421 Huron Avenue

1925–1928
427 Huron Avenue

Pearson, David J.

1868–1870
Harvard Square, corner Brattle Street

Peterson, John & Son

1914–1919
23 Church Street

Photo Reflex Studios

1931
14 Massachusetts Avenue

Pickles, Thomas H.

1892
385 Cambridge Street (Cambridge Street, between Columbia and Windsor streets)

1893–1894
585 Cambridge Street

Rand, Henry M.

1883
33 River Street (91 River Street)

(see also Rand & Taylor)

Rand & Taylor

1882
33 River Street (91 River Street)

(see also Henry M. Rand and F. J. Taylor & Company)

Rossiter, Peter E. G.

1944
44 Brattle Street

Sargent Studio

1944
1300 Massachusetts Avenue

Sarkisian, V. R. (Jake)

1899–1900
7 Boylston Street

Savoy Portrait Studio

1937–1944
1982 Massachusetts Avenue

Schivoiget, J. H. (also listed as Schlevoigt)

1893
310 Main Street (Main Street, between Portland and Albany streets)

Smith, George

1907
256 Elm Street

Spalding, Leland J.

1908
3 Boylston Street

Stearns, Walter H. & Company
1914
706 Massachusetts Avenue

Stevenson, James A.
1923–1925
524 Massachusetts Avenue
(see also James A. Stevenson & Company)

Stevenson, James A. & Company
1918–1919
7 Inman Square

Stimpson, John
1859
Wood's Block, Main Street (573 Massachusetts Avenue)

Story, Augustus
1876–1877
7 Brattle Street

Szczuka, Joseph
1920–1922
1056 Cambridge Street
(see also Luzackas & Szczuka, 1913)

Taylor, F. J. & Company
1883–1888
Main Street, corner Windsor Street
(see also Rand & Taylor)

Taylor, Herbert Whyte
1909–1927
349 Harvard Street

Taylor, Solatia M.
1928–1944
580 Massachusetts Avenue

Tinkham, Herbert C.
(see Tinkham & Woolway)

Tinkham & Woolway
1899
7 Haskell Street (Tinkham) and 11 Cleveland Street (Woolway)

1900
3 Clinton Street (Tinkham) and 11 Cleveland Street (Woolway)

Tupper, H. William (1846–1911)
1891–1900
Manager, Pach Brothers, 1181 Massachusetts Avenue

1901–1911
1388 Massachusetts Avenue
(see also Pach Brothers; Tupper Studio)

Tupper Studio
1912–1923
1388 Massachusetts Avenue
(see also Pach Brothers, William H. Tupper)

Umberhine, Frederick G.
(see Umberhine Studio)

Umberhine Studio
1918
559 Massachusetts Avenue

1919–1920
720 Massachusetts Avenue

University Studios (Benjamin M. Creedman, proprietor)
1941–1945
8 Boylston Street
(see also B. M. Creedman Studio)

Valin, John B.
1894–1896
310 Main Street (310 Massachusetts Avenue)

Warren, George K. (1834–1884)
1863–1864
449 Main Street (563 Massachusetts Avenue)

1865–1867
449 Main Street, Post Office Building (563 Massachusetts Avenue) and 459 Main Street, Wood's Building (573 Massachusetts Avenue)

1868–1870
449 Main Street (563 Massachusetts Avenue)

1871
449 Main Street (563 Massachusetts Avenue) and 145 Tremont Street, Boston

1872
559 Main Street (563 Massachusetts Avenue)

1873
559/563 Main Street (563 Massachusetts Avenue) and 289 Washington Street, Boston

1874
563 Main Street (563 Massachusetts Avenue)

1875
563 Main Street (563 Massachusetts Avenue) and 289 Washington Street, Boston

1876–1882
563 Main Street (563 Massachusetts Avenue) and 465 Washington Street, Boston

Webster, Maria M.
1911
631 Massachusetts Avenue
(see also Maurice M. Webster, Webster Studio)

Webster, Maurice M.
1910
631 Massachusetts Avenue

Webster Studio

1914–1916

631 Massachusetts Avenue (James T. Cox, 1914)

1917

649 Massachusetts Avenue

(see also James T. Cox, Maria M. Webster, Maurice M. Webster)

Whitney, George W.

(see Whitney & Son)

Whitney, Horace Webster

1882–1883

27 Central Square (5 Central Square)

(see also Whitney & Son)

Whitney & Son

1884–1917

563 Main Street (559 Massachusetts Avenue)

Williams, G. C.

1919

1093 Massachusetts Avenue

Wilmot, J. A.

1897

689 Cambridge Street

Wilson Magazine Company

1921–1922

1955 Massachusetts Avenue

1923

4 Cowperthwaite Street

1928–1944

1955 Massachusetts Avenue

Wing, Simon

1871

Harvard Square, corner Brattle Street

Winter, Charles, Jr.

1870

1 Hyde's Block, Main Street (633 Massachusetts Avenue)

(see also Harley, Metcalf & Winter)

Witter, Clarence E.

1919–1920

476 Massachusetts Avenue

Woiczak, J.

1916–1918

1056 Cambridge Street

Woolway, Frederick W.

(see Tinkham & Woolway)

Wootton, Silas E. L.

1904–1905

882 Main Street

Zack Bros. (Julius N. & Mayer H.)

1896

689 Cambridge Street

Zeeff, James

(see Apeda Photo Company)

Frederick C. Low Photographic Studio

Location: 5 Central Square
Date: 1884–1886
Photographer: Unknown
Source: Henry Deeks

Notman Photographic Company
Location: 1286 Massachusetts Avenue
Date: 1902–1904
Photographer: Unknown
Source: Harvard University Archives

84 *Pach Brothers Photographic Studio*

Location: 1181 Massachusetts Avenue
Date: 1906
Photographer: Boston Elevated Railway
Collection
Source: Cambridge Historical
Commission

85 **Former Studio of R. A. Dobson**
Location: 12 Brattle Street
Date: 1910
Photographer: Boston Elevated Railway
Collection
Source: Cambridge Historical
Commission

Notes

1

Between 1830 and 1850 Lowell's population rose from 6,074 to 33,383. In 1835, the population stood at about 13,000, and the industrial sector was growing rapidly. Owners of the Lowell cotton mills, in need of labor, promised jobs and security to those willing to move to the city.

2

As recorded in the Lowell City Directory of 1858, Lowell had 51 primary schools and 8 grammar schools, but only one high school serving 479 students, drawn from a population of 36,000 people. The prerequisites for high school admission were not very rigid, according to Henry A. Miles, in *Lowell As It Was and As It Is* (New York: Arno Press); a student had only to demonstrate a "good moral character" and the ability to read and write at a grammar-school level.

3

Florence T. Howe, "George Kendall Warren: His Agile Camera," *Yankee Magazine*, March 1959, p. 60.

4

William F. Robinson, *A Certain Slant of Light: The First Hundred Years of New England Photography* (Boston: New York Graphic Society), p. 25.

5

The Seventh Exhibition of the Massachusetts Charitable Mechanics Association at Faneuil and Quincy Halls, Boston, September and October, 1853.

6

The Eighth Exhibition of the Massachusetts Charitable Mechanics Association at Faneuil and Quincy Halls, Boston, September and October, 1856.

7

William Welling, *Photography in America: 1839–1900, The Formative Years* (New York: Thomas Y. Crowell Co.), p. 254.

8

"Candid" in this case means true-to-life portraits, not on-the-spot photographs, which were not possible until the twentieth century, when improved technology permitted short enough exposure time to allow for a "candid" in the modern sense.

9

Welling, *Photography in America*, p. 254.

10

Harvard Crimson, July 3, 1877, p. 110.

11

From the catalogue card on Warren's photographs at the Boston Athenaeum.

12

Howe, "George Kendall Warren," p. 61.

13

Robinson, *A Certain Slant of Light*, p. 108.

14

The Thirteenth Exhibition of the Massachusetts Charitable Mechanics Association at Park Square, Boston, September and October, 1878.

Bibliography

Government Reports and Records

Baldwin, Thomas W. *Vital Records of Cambridge, Massachusetts to the Year 1850.* 2 vols. Boston, 1914–1915.

Cambridge Historical Commission, survey files, 1964–1983.

Cambridge Park Department, Annual Reports, 1893–1900.

Census of the United States. 1860–1900.

Massachusetts Department of Vital Statistics. Boston.

Middlesex County Registry of Deeds. Land Records.

Middlesex County Registry of Probate. Probate Records.

General References

Almy, Charles. "The History of the Third District Court of Eastern Middlesex," *Cambridge Historical Society Proceedings.* Vol. 17 (1923–1924), pp. 16–27.

Bacon, George F. *Cambridgeport: Its Representative Business Men, and Its Points of Interest.* Newark, N.J., 1892.

Bail, Hamilton Vaughan. *Views of Harvard: A Pictorial Record to 1860.* Cambridge, 1949.

Batchelder, Samuel F. *Bits of Cambridge History.* Cambridge, 1930.

Batchelder, Samuel Francis. "The Washington Elm Tradition," *Cambridge Historical Society Proceedings.* Vol. 18 (1925), pp. 46–75.

Boston Directories. 1870–1945.

Boston Transcript. Obituaries.

Cambridge Chronicle. 1846–1983.

Cambridge Chronicle Hundredth Anniversary Edition. Cambridge, 1946.

Cambridge Chronicle Semi-Centennial Souvenir. Cambridge, 1896.

Cambridge Chronicle Seventy-Fifth Anniversary. Cambridge, 1921.

Cambridge Directories. Published annually with occasional exceptions, 1848–1972.

Cambridge Easter Magazine. Cambridge, 1914.

Cambridge Historical Commission. *Survey of Architectural History in Cambridge, Report One: East Cambridge.* Cambridge, 1965. *Report Two: Mid Cambridge.* By Antoinette Downing, Elisabeth MacDougall, and Eleanor Pearson. Cambridge, 1967. *Report Three: Cambridgeport.* Cambridge, 1971. *Report Four: Old Cambridge.* By Bainbridge Bunting and Robert H. Nylander. Cambridge, 1973. *Report Five: Northwest Cambridge.* By Arthur Krim. Cambridge, 1977.

Cambridge Tribune. 1878–1941.

Cambridge Tribune Semi-Centennial: 1846–1896. Cambridge, 1896.

Cambridge Tribune Souvenir Number. Cambridge, 1890

Canfield, C. W. "Notes on Photography in Boston in 1839–40," *The American Annual of Photography* (1894), pp. 261–262.

Emmet, Alan. *Cambridge, Massachusetts: The Changing of a Landscape.* Cambridge, 1978.

Exhibitions of the Massachusetts Charitable Mechanics Association. 1833–1884.

Fay, Spofford and Thorndike. Office Archives.

Flagg, Wilson, *The Woods and Byways of New England.* Boston, 1872.

First Church Congregational. Archives.

Foxcroft, Frank. "No-License in Cambridge," *Cambridge Historical Society Proceedings.* Vol. 13 (1918), pp. 9–16.

Gilman, Arthur, ed. *The Cambridge of Eighteen Hundred and Ninety-Six.* Cambridge, 1896.

Gozzaldi, Mary Isabella. "Merchants of Old Cambridge in the Early Days," *Cambridge Historical Society Proceedings.* Vol. 8 (1913), pp. 30–40.

Gras, N. S. B. *Harvard Co-operative Society Past and Present: 1882–1942.* Cambridge, 1942.

Greene, Harding U. "The History of the Utilities in Cambridge," *Cambridge Historical Society Proceedings.* Vol. 42 (1972), pp. 7–13.

Harvard Class Albums. Cambridge, 1860–1900.

Harvard College Class of 1888. *Secretary's Report.* Nos. 1–8. Cambridge, 1889–1920.

Harvard Square Business Men's Association. "Petition for the Removal of the Surface Structures Used in Connection with the Cambridge Subway in Harvard Square." c. 1923.

Hastings, Lewis Morey. "The Streets of Cambridge, Their Origin and History," *Cambridge Historical Society Proceedings.* Vol. 14 (1919), pp. 31–78.

Howe, Florence T. "George Kendall Warren: His Agile Camera," *Yankee Magazine,* March 1959.

Howe, Lois Lilley. "Harvard Square in the 'Seventies and 'Eighties," *Cambridge Historical Society Proceedings.* Vol. 30 (1944), pp. 11–27.

Hoyle, Pamela. *The Boston Ambience, an Exhibition of Nineteenth-Century Photographs.* Boston, 1981.

Hoyle, Pamela. *The Development of Photography in Boston, 1840–1875.* Boston, 1979.

Ingersoll, Ernest. "Harvard's Botanic Garden and Its Botanist," *The Century,* Vol. 32 (1886), pp. 237–248.

Lowell Directories. 1855–1866.

"The Memorial of John Harvard: October 15, 1884." Cambridge, 1884.

Morrison, Samuel Eliot. *Three Centuries of Harvard.* Cambridge, 1936.

Newhall, Beaumont. *The Daguerreotype in America.* New York, 1976.

Newhall, Beaumont. *The History of Photography.* New York, 1964.

Paige, Lucius R. *History of Cambridge, Massachusetts, 1630–1877, with a Genealogical Register.* Boston, 1877. *Supplement and Index.* Mary Isabella Gozzaldi. Cambridge, 1930.

Palmer, Foster M. "Horse Car, Trolley and Subway," *Cambridge Historical Society Proceedings.* Vol. 39 (1962), pp. 78–107.

Photo Era Magazine. Boston, 1891–1900.

Reiff, Daniel D. "Harvard's Memorial Hall and its Tower," *Victorian Society in America Newsletter,* Spring/Summer 1973, Philadelphia.

Rindge Technical School. *After Fifty Years Rindge Technical School, 1888–1938.* Cambridge, 1938.

Robinson, William F. *A Certain Slant of Light.* Boston, 1980.

Stillman, W. J., ed. *Poetic Localities of Cambridge.* Boston, 1876.

Sutherland, Arthur E. "The Harvard Law School's Four Oldest Houses," *Cambridge Historical Society Proceedings.* Vol. 41 (1967–1969), pp. 117–131.

Sutton, S. B. *Cambridge Reconsidered.* Cambridge, 1976.

Taft, Robert. *Photography and the American Scene.* New York, 1964.

Vogel, Susan Maycock. "Hartwell and Richardson: An Introduction to their Work," *Journal of the Society of Architectural Historians,* May 1973, pp. 132–146.

Welling, William. *Photography in America: 1839–1900, The Formative Years.* New York, 1978.

Wells, James A. *A History of the Old Cambridge Photographic Club.* Boston, 1905.

Wilson's Photographic Magazine (The Philadelphia Photographer). 1865–1867.

Wood, John W. "Cambridgeport: A Brief History," *Cambridge Historical Society Proceedings.* Vol. 35 (1953–1954), 79–90.

Wright, George Grier. "Gleanings from Early Cambridge Directories," *Cambridge Historical Society Proceedings.* Vol. 15 (1920–1921), pp. 30–40.